D1521611

TEACHER SUPERVISION THAT WORKS

TEACHER SUPERVISION THAT WORKS

A Guide for University Supervisors

DEBRA J. ANDERSON
ROBERT L. MAJOR
RICHARD R. MITCHELL

PRAEGER

New York
Westport, Connecticut
London

Library of Congress Cataloging-in-Publication Data

Anderson, Debra J.
    Teacher supervision that works : a guide for university
supervisors / Debra J. Anderson, Robert L. Major, and Richard R.
Mitchell.
        p.   cm.
    Includes bibliographical references (p.   ) and index.
    ISBN 0–275–94264–3 (alk. paper)
    1. Student teachers—Supervision of—United States.
    I. Major, Robert L.   II. Mitchell, Richard R.   III. Title.
LB2157.U5A75   1992
370'.7'33—dc20   91–39696

British Library Cataloguing in Publication Data is available.

Library of Congress Catalog Card Number: 91–39696
ISBN: 0–275–94264–3

First published in 1992

Praeger Publishers, One Madison Avenue, New York, NY 10010
An imprint of Greenwood Publishing Group, Inc.

Printed in the United States of America

The paper used in this book complies with the
Permanent Paper Standard issued by the National
Information Standards Organization (Z39.48–1984).

10 9 8 7 6 5 4 3 2 1

To our mentors at the University of Northern Colorado,
who believed in quality student teacher supervision.

Contents

Preface

> The college supervisor has a critical and central role in the program of teacher education; the assignment of that role should not be made lightly.
>
> Florence B. Stratemeyer

Florence B. Stratemeyer's 1964 statement is even more true today. The need for outstanding university supervisors who balance the needs and interests of the student, the university, and the K–12 school has never been greater. They are the link between institutions of higher learning and public and private schools. The strength of this very fragile link is determined by how well supervisors are prepared for their role. A knowledgeable supervisor who can objectively help the student teacher and represent the university while remaining sensitive to the needs of both the cooperating teacher and the cooperating school is the epitome of a university supervisor. Such a supervisor *does* make a difference!

Teachers impact, for good or evil, thousands during their careers. How they interact with students, what values they pass on, what learnings they deem important—these and countless attitudes are internalized during student teaching.

Student teachers are always on someone else's turf. They are vulnerable. Perhaps this explains why they are so pliable, so capable of learning vast amounts of material in a short period, so receptive to life-shaping change, and so in need of a well-prepared university supervisor. Student teachers must be exposed to the best the university has to offer.

Teacher Supervision That Works: A Guide for University Supervisors is intended as a practical guide for university supervisors but could easily serve as a text for mentors and cooperating teachers. It examines the supervisory process, the preparation necessary for supervision, the responsibilities of the university supervisor, the historical assumption underlying the supervisory role, and what research tells us about effective supervision.

The authors hope that novice and veteran supervisors and cooperating teachers will use this book to better understand supervision and apply the concepts to help student teachers become the best teachers they are capable of becoming.

TEACHER
SUPERVISION
THAT
WORKS

Chapter 1

Realities and Misconceptions Surrounding University Supervision

We believe that three realities and two misconceptions surround university supervision.

REALITY NUMBER ONE

The first reality is that it takes a special talent and intelligence to be an effective university supervisor. Everyone can talk a good game of supervision, but not all can do it. There is a big difference between going through the motions of supervision and supervising in ways that make a difference.

Student teachers must satisfy at least two strangers while on their voyage into the unknown, and they need moral and technical support. University supervisors must be effective listeners and perceptive observers. They must be able to recognize and communicate the complex characteristics of learning and teaching. They must be able to give criticism and praise in ways that make a positive contribution. They must know when to stand firm and when to bend and tread lightly. They must recognize problems that need immediate attention and differentiate them from those that will take care of themselves. They must also be aware that attitudes not acted out are as important as behaviors expressed.

Teaching is complicated, and there are an infinite number of ways a teacher can act and react. Teaching is also intimate and personal. Outstanding teachers frequently do not know why they behave as they do. They often do what they do because it feels or seems right.

As compared with average teachers, outstanding teachers generally do such things as demonstrate a greater tolerance for silence, encourage more student questions, and criticize less, but teaching cannot be "cookbooked"! One interaction analysis system or even a series of such systems will not adequately assess outstanding teaching, nor will check sheets, lists, or systematic research-based evaluation tools. Teaching is much too complicated.

Long ago, Dwight W. Allen's (1966) *Microteaching* and James M. Cooper's (1971) *Technical Skills of Teaching* made a contribution, as did Amidon's (1965) *Verbal Behavior of Superior Teachers*, Arno Bellack's (1966) *Pedagogical Moves*, and Charles Galloway's (1962) *Nonverbal Communication* (and they still make a contribution today), but no system or idea alone, even the most recent from such scholars and researchers as Lee S. Shulman (1987) and Lauren B. Resnick (1987), can begin to cover what an outstanding teacher does. Nor can a video camera capture the wide and varied range of teacher behaviors—the subtle winks and touches, the smiles and the written words of praise. Nor can it pick up all the work and tears that go into creating a classroom that beckons children and tells them that they are safe. It cannot grasp the lasting impressions made by whispered words of encouragement and quiet gestures that say *all right! Great!* University supervisors must be alert, sensitive, and bright enough to recognize outstanding teaching when they see it, and they must be humble enough to say to themselves, *every day*, "If I were teaching in the classroom in which I'm now observing, what kind of person would I like evaluating me?"

REALITY NUMBER TWO

The second reality is that when you work with a very gifted cooperating teacher and a very talented student teacher, you often feel unneeded.

This should not have to be the case. Help these gifted student teachers recognize teachable moments; teach them to use only the best examples; encourage them to make what they teach more relevant; challenge them to begin mastering the art of asking questions; prompt them to keep improving upon complicated methods, such as the classroom discussion; and help them to understand that teaching is a professional commitment for life, and effective teachers are made over a period of years.

Early in the term, observe student teachers from the point of view of a parent and tell them why you would want your child in their class. Observe them from the point of view of a superintendent and explain why you would hire them. Feel free to use formal interaction analysis systems such as Flanders's (1967) *Interaction Analysis Categories*. Student teachers are capable of using as much feedback as you are able to give. You might even suggest they make, for future use, a video recording of themselves introducing a unit or presenting a lab demonstration.

It can be a joy to work with these gifted students. You do not always have to hold back, and you can work with them on strategies some supervisors reserve for graduate students and in-service teachers (e.g., Madeline Hunter's (1982) *Essential Elements of Successful Instruction*). The very best student teachers need assistance with management, appropriate use of questions in the classroom, making transitions from activity to activity and so forth. Do not feel left out and useless. Your talented student teachers need as much reinforcement as anyone, can improve as much as anyone, and need to see you as much as anyone.

REALITY NUMBER THREE

The third reality of university supervision is that the work of the university supervisor should be respected.

Twenty-five years ago, Florence Stratemeyer (1964), a professor at Teachers College Columbia University and past president of the Association of Teacher Educators, wrote: "The college supervisor has a critical and central role in the program of teacher education. The assignment of that role should not be made lightly" (Association for Student Teaching, p. 163). At about this time, Dorothy McGeogh (1967) and Margaret Lindsey (1969), also professors at Teachers College and also past presidents of

ATE, were saying much the same thing. We believed them then and feel their words are even more true today.

The reality is, however, that some university faculty and administrators see supervision as neither central, critical, nor important. Instead, some see the university supervisor as one who consumes a lot of the budget, driving aimlessly from school to school.

Yet we contend that only the most flexible, intelligent, talented, and courageous can be university supervisors. University supervisors must be knowledgeable, for they are open to any question at any time. It is not uncommon to be asked thirty or forty different questions each day: When will student loans be ready? Are my students normal? How should I handle swearing? My cooperating teacher never leaves the room; what should I do? How could your university send us such an ill-prepared student teacher? My teacher thinks Madeline Hunter is way off base but I disagree; what should I do? Our school uses assertive discipline, but I think it treats kids like dogs, pigeons, and mice; am I wrong? And on and on. Supervisors cannot gain time to think by asking the class what it believes about an issue, nor can they say, "We'll be covering this next week."

It takes patience to work with cooperating teachers who do not share your philosophy and who think out loud. It takes the ability to provide a specific, objective analysis of the student teacher's performance to conduct an effective conference. And it takes knowing how to lead a discussion; how to word and reword higher-order questions; how to help students clarify their thinking; and how to create an atmosphere of trust to conduct a worthwhile seminar.

In addition, it takes a special person to tell student teachers that they have not done an acceptable job of student teaching and should not enter the teaching profession. And it takes a perceptive and levelheaded person to keep in mind, while cushioning such news, that these individuals, who seem to be failing now, will undoubtedly enter a helping profession, be taxpayers, parents, voters, and perhaps even school board members. We want and will need their support. They are still human beings and deserve to leave student teaching with as much dignity and self-worth as possible.

Not everyone is flexible or sensitive or caring enough to be an effective university supervisor. Your job is most important and takes an enormous amount of talent!

MISCONCEPTION NUMBER ONE

The first misconception surrounding university supervision is that anyone with recent teaching experience who is at least working toward a master's degree can be an effective university supervisor.

Although some universities operate as if this were the case, the truth of the matter is that not all good teachers can be good cooperating teachers, let alone good university supervisors.

Some teachers, even very effective teachers, fall apart when they become cooperating teachers. They coddle their student teachers, try to make them their clone, head off all signs of failure, give too much input too early, and do not listen enough. Others are myopic or jump to premature conclusions or lack empathy. If such persons were suddenly given the responsibility of working with ten different administrators, twenty developing student teachers, and forty independent cooperating teachers, it might become quite frustrating for everyone. It is true that many effective teachers make effective cooperating teachers, but it is also true that some do not.

The same, we believe, can be said for those who make the transition from being effective cooperating teachers to being effective university supervisors. Some are able to transfer their skills and can work well with adults and those having wide ranges of abilities and personalities. These persons can be effective university supervisors. Others, because they do not have enough abilities to transfer or cannot make the transition, will not become successful. Not everyone can be a university supervisor.

MISCONCEPTION NUMBER TWO

The second misconception surrounding university supervision is that teacher education will be improved if university supervisors return to the classroom as a teacher every few years.

Those who believe that major teacher education problems will be solved by such action need to realize that university supervisors are in the schools every day. They have not stayed the same as they were twenty-five years ago. University supervisors see the latest materials and hardware and know how they are being used. Very few new methods or techniques go unnoticed by university supervisors.

University supervisors see the beginnings of classes and the endings of school days, the detention rooms, and students passing in the halls. They hear the announcements, visit the lounges, and see gifted teachers using the latest techniques with today's children on a daily basis. Their views are not skewed by having taught only one group of students, in one classroom, in one district.

Those who believe that teacher education can be improved by sending university supervisors back into the classroom need to realize that the same kinds of caring people of yesterday who stood at the door to say hello to students each period, knew their students' names and used them, respected students' ideas and sought their advice, and understood that each student is unique, would be just as effective today. Effective teaching then is still effective teaching today, and it will be effective teaching tomorrow.

Twenty-five years ago, it took a dedicated teacher to treat every student as a special person. It took a devoted teacher to help each student appreciate his or her own uniqueness. It took energy to be pleasant and patience to listen. It took a teacher who placed a high value upon allowing nature to pull and tug each individual toward becoming all he or she could become. It still takes that kind of teacher today. University supervisors have not lost these attitudes and skills. They teach seminars each week, and many teach during the summer. (Most of those we know, however, would welcome an opportunity to teach for a week or month or term in a K–12 classroom.)

And, finally, those demanding that university supervisors return to the classroom because students have changed since they have last taught need to realize that students are basically the same as they were twenty-five years ago. Today's students still have crushes, pimples, irrational fears, and primp for hours.

Eighth graders continue to think they are grown up; fifth graders are still full of questions; and most third graders, as in the past, like school.

When you read books by Horace Mann (1844), Walter R. Smith (1924), Emerson E. White (1893), Jesse B. Sears (1928), Levi Seeley (1903), and others, works written 60 or 90 or even 150 years ago, you realize that students are students. They all have aspirations. They all are a bit insecure. They need to grow and learn. They are searching to discover themselves. They love and hate and get angry and are selfish. They all use poor judgment at times, yet turn around and show moments of maturity beyond their years. They are idealistic and impatient but also have a sense of fair play unequaled by adults. They need to be liked, to feel important, to feel they can make a contribution.

Students tend to remain the same as they were before the age of motion pictures, radio, and television. Their staying the same may not always seem to be so, but this is only because we now hear about every desperate, brutal, and rage-filled act, regardless of where it occurs. Students, like most of us, simply live and move with our changing world, feeling at times that they have no control at all.

Be proud you are a university supervisor. You are a member of an influential profession; and because you instill attitudes and values in budding professionals, professionals who will influence thousands for decades, your job is most important.

An Historical Overview of University Supervision

Supervision as a part of teacher preparation is not new. It has been around for as long as individuals have attempted to help others teach. To appreciate the art of supervision and comprehend the magnitude of this process, we must understand its history and development.

Supervision has always been an integral part of teacher education. In Europe, recorded formal teacher preparation began in 1439, the date generally accepted as the establishment of the earliest teacher training institution of Godshead College in England. This program gave students an opportunity to teach demonstration lessons to each other (Johnson & Perry, 1969, p. 1).

On the European continent, supervision was not officially established until 1672 when the first professional teacher training center opened at Lyons, France. This program emphasized what to teach *and* how to teach it. Thirteen years later, in 1685, at Rheims, France, Jean Bapiste De LaSalle established the first normal school (Johnson & Perry, 1969, p. 2). Other schools, patterned after the normal school, followed throughout Europe.

Most of the settlers of the East Coast of what was to become the United States came from northern Europe. They brought with them a concept of formal education. Survival was the foremost concern in the new settlements. Education had to wait until there was time to concentrate on other things beyond food, clothing, shelter, and personal safety. Formal teacher education was slow in coming to the United States. Initially, teachers were those who could read, write, and do simple sums. Most were not formally trained except for those who had the privilege of tutelage or a European education.

There were few institutions that prepared teachers. In fact, the first normal school was not established until 1823. It was a three-year seminary developed by Samuel Hall in Concord, Vermont. From the beginning, town children were admitted and taught demonstration lessons by the teachers of the school. Also from the beginning, normal school students, after observing, were then permitted to "practice teach" these same children (Johnson & Perry, 1969, p. 3).

Following the establishment of the first normal school, teacher education progressed slowly. Sixteen years later, in 1839, stimulated by a pledge of $10,000 from Edmund Dwight, a Boston merchant, the state of Massachusetts established a teacher training center. In the next ten years, additional normal schools were developed in New York, Connecticut, and Massachusetts.

One of the first normal schools in the Midwest, the sixth in the United States, was Ypsilanti Normal School. It opened in Ypsilanti, Michigan, in 1850. This normal school also had a model school. The model school gave advanced teacher education students an opportunity to work with students in a practice teaching situation. Each normal school teacher education student in the practice teaching program was responsible for one recitation daily for the entire term. During the term the teacher education students were supervised by the normal school staff who required them to make detailed reports of their work (Johnson & Perry, 1969, p. 6).

Just prior to the Civil War, teacher education in the United States received a much needed stimulus from Dr. Edward A. Sheldon, who established the Oswego School in Oswego, New York, in 1861. He introduced the formalized Pestalozzian methods of instruction (Blair, Curtis, & Moon, 1958, pp. 4–5). These methods centered around teaching techniques that did not violate the natural growth patterns of children, were pupil-centered as opposed to teacher-centered, and focused on learning by doing (Dupuis, 1966, p. 108).

After the Civil War, the normal school movement, with its emphasis on observation, participation, and practice teaching, grew rapidly. By 1874 it was reported by the United States commissioner of education that sixty-seven state normal schools had been established, forty-seven of which contained laboratory schools (Perrodine, 1955, p. 6).

Another phase of the normal school movement that played an important part in the development of the student teaching program took place in Bloomington, Illinois, in 1855. "A group of students from the Normal traveled to Germany, where they came into contact with the ideas of Johann Friedrich Herbart. These students . . . returned to Bloomington Normal as teachers and brought many of Herbart's ideas with them" (Johnson & Perry, 1969, p. 5). The emphasis of Herbart's concept was the method of presentation written in specific form. A lesson included five steps. They were preparation, presentation, comparison, generalization, and application. Supervised practice teaching was heavily stressed.

By the last decade of the nineteenth century, most normal schools had developed a system of supervised practice teaching as an integral part of preparing teachers. One of the major problems encountered, however, was the quality of supervision. Another problem was finding opportunities for aspiring teachers to work directly with children. When school districts were approached by normal school personnel with a request to place teacher trainees in local districts for the purpose of gaining direct classroom teaching experience, many local districts declined. Parents in those districts did not want their children practiced upon. Also, there were questions about the appropriate method(s) to be used and about classroom ownership.

During the last decade of the nineteenth century, there was controversy over qualifications of those who would serve as classroom supervisors. Teacher trainers who had been schooled in the philosophy and methodology of Pestalozzi, Herbart, the Lancastrian movement, and others stressed that students should do their practice teaching under the guidance and supervision of one trained in the same method or discipline. This led to problems. If local districts were satisfied with their success in educating children, why should they change their operation to satisfy teacher training institutions? Why should local districts let college liberals experiment on their children, especially since local districts were already suspicious of "foreign ideas." After all, Pestalozzi was a Swiss, Herbart a Prussian, and the Lancastrian method was English.

This lack of communication, understanding, cooperation, and trust between local school districts and teacher training institutions stimulated the development and growth of laboratory schools. The laboratory schools were part of the college or university, staffed by teachers trained in the methodology endorsed by teaching faculty. They were usually located on or adjacent to the campus. In the laboratory schools, supervision could be controlled by teachers trained in the same methodology as the students. Cubberly (1934) reported: "By 1910, there were approximately 200 public normal schools and 75 private normal schools in the United States" (p. 354). Five years later, G. E. Walk (1917) concluded in a study of sixty representative state normal schools that 78 percent maintained their own laboratory schools, while 22 percent used cooperating schools (pp. 69–84). The emphasis in education at that time was on close supervision to ensure that the proper teaching methods and techniques were employed at the proper time. (It is doubtful that the term "cloning" was in vogue then, but the message is clear.)

In the first twenty-five years of the twentieth century, two professional organizations strongly advocated supervision of students in a clinical setting. One, the Association of Teacher Colleges, created in 1917, believed that supervision in a clinical setting should be more strongly mandated. It adopted policies in 1926 advocating the establishment and maintenance of a laboratory school for observation, demonstration, and supervised student teaching as part of each teacher training institution. It also recognized that student teaching requirements could be satisfied by experiences that took place in urban or rural schools (Williams, 1942, p. 11). A second organization, the National Association of Directors of Supervised Student Teaching, was created in 1920. It recognized that all professionals involved in student teaching should be included in its membership. Two years later membership was opened to persons whose work was directly concerned with supervised teaching as a critical part of the training of teachers. In 1922, to reflect the new membership, the name of the organization was changed to the National Association of Supervisors of Student Teaching. The first yearbook was published in 1924.

From 1910 to 1925, the majority of those training as teachers, at least in state normal schools or in state teacher colleges, received some form of supervised clinical experience. Usually it was in the form of supervised practice teaching.

At this time, other important changes in the educational process were taking place. State licensure or certification of teachers became widespread; secondary teachers, who had been previously trained in the disciplines only, were now being trained in state teacher colleges rather than in the universities; and qualification for a state teaching license required trainees to become involved in the teacher training programs. This requirement included a clinical experience called student teaching. This change created a rapid increase in enrollment in teacher training programs and called for the expansion of the laboratory school facilities and staff. While many laboratory schools did expand, some did not and were forced to ask public schools to accept student teachers.

During this era of laboratory schools in the first half of the twentieth century, at least five types were created. Each laboratory school was labeled as one of the following: (1) a practice school; (2) a model school; (3) a training school; (4) a demonstration school; or (5) an experimental school. They did not emerge chronologically or in any particular order. They developed to fulfill a need as determined by the direction of the respective institutions or focus of the particular teacher education program.

The "practice school" was one of the first laboratory schools. It was a place to practice a specific method and, as such, had many qualities of an apprenticeship program.

The "model school" offered a model for associated public schools and their teachers to follow. It taught through demonstration and observation. The model school tended to follow a particular philosophy of education, such as the Pestalozzian method.

The "training school" had basically the same organizational structure as public schools of the time. The schools were designed so that "the focus was on the development of patterns of instruction that could be so standardized that anyone, regardless of preparation and experience, could use them effectively, showing a close resemblance to the lessons used in both the Practice and Model Schools" (Blair, Curtis, & Moon, 1958, p. 5).

The "demonstration school" reflected the Herbartian method. It focused on the philosophy of academic disciplines taught by emphasizing the proper teaching methods and strategies that were incorporated into the lesson plan. A major part of the direct experience of the student teacher was (1) to make a concentrated study of previously prepared master lessons; (2) to see these lessons demonstrated in the classroom by the teachers of the demonstration school; and (3) to teach the same lesson during the period of student teaching with strict attention to the details of the prepared plans (Blair, Curtis, & Moon, 1958, p. 6).

The "experimental school," or child study school, dealt with insight and basic knowledge involved in the learning process. The teachers played an integral part in the decision-making process concerning curriculum, methodology, texts to be used, and the form of discipline to be emphasized in the classroom. One new concept was that students should have a role in the planning of their respective education. Due to the nature of the schools and the freedom involved, it is no wonder that most experimental schools included graduate students as part of their programs. These graduate students were trained "to be master teachers, teachers of special methods, or specialists in education" (Blair, Curtis, & Moon, 1958, p. 7).

Constant supervision was one advantage of the "laboratory school." Student teachers were able to observe experts and be critics in a clinical situation. Another advantage was that since laboratory school graduates became teachers in public school programs across the nation, public school systems were able to pick and choose from a variety of graduates, and if so desired, to develop an eclectic approach in their districts.

One disadvantage of the laboratory school system was the inbreeding of faculties in laboratory schools. The students involved in the teacher education process did not receive the benefit of a diverse training. They were considered well prepared to follow a specific approach but were in trouble if they were unable to adapt to the methodology used in the local district in which they were student teaching. (The same can be said today for some institutions that stress one specific method for elementary mathematics, reading, and other subjects in their teacher training programs.)

As the need for teachers at both the elementary and secondary school levels grew during the 1930s and 1940s, laboratory schools, because of their size and budgets, found it more difficult to accommodate the increasing numbers of students seeking teacher certification or licensure. By now, observation, participation, and student teaching were integral parts of teacher certification programs, and an increasing number of teacher training institutions deemed it necessary to ask public school personnel to provide clinical experiences.

As long as the programs were conducted in laboratory or adjacent public schools, supervision of clinical experiences was not a problem. One problem for the supervising staff, however, was the inconvenience of leaving the laboratory school and traveling to the host public school. As the need for additional cooperating public and private schools increased, the distance from the local laboratory schools also increased. That posed a very real problem for those involved in supervisory activities. Supervisors simply could not be in two places at the same time. There were two distinct options. One was to limit the teacher education program to fit existing facilities. The other was to create a new full-time position—namely, the university or college student teacher supervisor.

In 1946, the National Association of Supervisors of Student Teaching, an organization that had been created to promote organized student teacher supervision, had its first post–World War II convention. At the convention, an amendment to the constitution was made. It stated that "Membership . . . shall include persons in all types of institutions engaged in teacher education whose work is concerned with the organization and supervision of student teaching, broadly defined" (Patterson, McGeogh, & Olson, 1958, p. 3). Also, the name was changed to the Association for Student Teaching, reflecting the new membership.

Three other organizations drew public attention to teacher preparation. They were: (1) the American Association of Teachers Colleges through a study called "School and Community Laboratory Experiences in Teacher Education"; (2) the National Commission on Teacher Education and Professional Standards through its emphasis on raising the standards of the teaching profession; and (3) the Progressive Education Association through its philosophy of concern for the "whole child" (Haines, 1962, p. 27).

One major point during the post–World War II period was to lengthen and enrich the period of supervised student teaching. This, however, posed new problems for those involved in the scheduling of student teacher placements. As the number of days and hours required in the classrooms increased to accommodate certification or licensure requirements, there was an increased need for more classroom supervisors. This problem was compounded by rapidly increasing numbers of students needing student teaching experience. More public schools were required to provide that opportunity. As a result, sites for the student teaching experiences were being located further from campus, making supervision by the teacher education staff more difficult, if not impossible. The college and university education departments were facing problems similar to those that their predecessors in the laboratory schools faced in earlier decades.

Initially, the college or university representatives supervising student teachers were faculty members from the College of Education. They usually supervised student teachers and taught one or more classes in professional education. As teacher education programs expanded to include student teachers in secondary education, members of the academic disciplines became involved in the supervisory process, usually in conjunction with the university's Department of Education. As distances increased between host public schools and academic institutions, logistical problems seemed to multiply. It became difficult for academic supervisors to serve two masters. When a student teacher had a problem that needed immediate input from the university supervisor, which program—teaching or supervision—would receive priority treatment? All too often, the visible, on-campus class received the attention.

Smaller state and private institutions seemed to have fewer problems. First, there was the closeness of their *faculties*. Second, they had smaller numbers of students with which to deal. Larger institutions, usually state colleges and universities, however, seemed to have more problems and moved either toward full-time supervision of student teachers or toward the use of resident teachers on a full-time basis. They had the freedom to change their schedules to meet immediate problems as they occurred. As the second half of the twentieth century progressed, the numbers of full-time supervisors in state colleges and universities increased rapidly.

Supervision grew and expanded as a process and a profession throughout the 1960s. The school population continued to grow. New public elementary and secondary schools continued to increase in number. Even though more educational programs were being funded by state and federal sources, the teacher shortage remained.

In the early 1970s, however, the population of school-age students began to decline rapidly. Sources and support for special programs disappeared or were limited as federal and state budgets were closely scrutinized. The demand for teachers evaporated. Many districts eliminated entire programs, beginning with those that were elective or expensive. In many instances, staff positions in host schools were cut. Individuals with twelve to fifteen years' seniority were released or put on unrequested leave. The effect on the host schools was devastating.

The ripple effect hit the teacher education programs at colleges and universities with similar results. By the mid-1970s, enrollment in teacher training programs dropped drastically. The last staff members hired were the first released. Since programs within the university are funded on a basis of student enrollment, financial support for teacher education programs decreased rapidly. All expensive services were questioned. Because supervision of student teachers included travel, supervisory services were reduced. Many full-time supervisors assumed other responsibilities such as teaching core courses in the teacher education programs. For a period of ten to fifteen years, supervision of student teacher services was reduced or severely curtailed.

Today, we are faced with many of the old problems and some new ones. The preschool population is increasing, teachers are in demand in urban areas and the Sun Belt, and teacher education programs, particularly in elementary education, are increasing.

University supervisors can have a definite and lasting influence on those who will become teachers. The university supervisor is present during one of the most exciting times a teacher will ever know—that of becoming a professional. University supervisors are there when student teachers face the reality that teaching is a most demanding profession requiring tenacity, dedication, and a willingness to work closely with others. Most professionals in teaching have to wait years to see significant change in their students. University supervisors are often privileged to observe the metamorphosis of a student becoming a teacher in only three or four months. That reward makes all the rest worthwhile.

Chapter 3 _____

Preparation of the University Supervisor: Documenting the Need, Attitudes, Experiences, Skills, and Attributes

The preparation of university supervisors cannot be taken lightly. Well-prepared supervisors contribute to the development of well-prepared beginning teachers. This chapter presents a documentation of the need for well-prepared university supervisors and an overview of the attitudes, experiences, skills, and attributes needed for effective supervision.

DOCUMENTATION OF NEED

Literature addressing the preparation required for effective university supervisors is almost nonexistent. This is true of related topics as well. For example, topics such as the knowledge, beliefs, and judgment criteria of supervisors (Simmons, 1988) and studies concentrating wholly upon the university supervisor (Marrou, 1988) have not been extensively researched or documented. We may speculate why this is so.

Troyer (1986) lists a variety of reasons illustrating why the focus of researchers has excluded university supervisors. She states:

Perhaps we are fearful that common criticism of teacher education will be substantiated, or that additional criticism will be forthcoming as a result of new findings. Perhaps we are hesitant to consign a complex and divergent population with whom we identify so closely to the few lines of simplistic findings that may result from some research efforts or, perhaps we perceive research on teacher educators as less salient than other lines of educational inquiry. (p. 6)

Another reason for the lack of literature on supervisors may be that "the perceived nature of supervision is a low priority task with little benefit in academia" (Simmons, 1988, p. 6). This attitude is substantiated in part by data obtained from a national survey of preservice teacher education in the United States. Bowman (1978) reports:

Teacher preparation institutions have often been accused (by their own students as well as by public school personnel) of showing a lack of concern for the competency of supervisors of student teachers. (p. 5)

In other words, it may be that few in higher education, including some teacher educators, understand the complex nature and importance of supervision. In an era of increased accountability, we must question the priorities of teacher preparation institutions that fail to place importance upon supervision.

Concern for the need for well-prepared supervisors has been indicated by contemporary educators. In 1988, Marrou asserted:

If teacher training institutions are going to prepare student teachers effectively for the classroom, they must first thoroughly prepare their first line of defense—their university supervisors. (p. 13)

Also to illustrate the need for supervisory training, Zeichner and Liston (1987) describe problems encountered in their program. They stated:

The supervisors in the program are graduate students in the Department of Curriculum and Instruction who spend anywhere from one to five years working in the program. From our experience, it takes a few semesters to prepare supervisors to work in a program such as this, and particularly for them to develop the expertise to be effective in implementing the inquiry and reflective aspects of this program. Frequently, as soon as supervisors have begun to make sufficient progress in the development of supervisory and pedagogical strategies, they leave, and work must begin to prepare a new group of individuals for supervisory roles. (p. 42)

It is evident from this statement that Zeichner and Liston believe supervisors need to be prepared for their new role.

Since 1980, enrollment in elementary and secondary teacher education programs has increased. However, decreased funding for teacher education programs and a smaller pool of eligible doctoral graduates have resulted in the hiring of faculty unprepared to supervise student teachers. Unfortunately, in some institutions, supervision seems to be the first program trimmed under a tightening budget.

We wonder if those who make such personnel decisions for supervision programs have thought about the long-term consequences of their actions. Do they know that "the quality of any teacher education program is at least partially dependent upon the quality of its professoriate" (Troyer, 1986, p. 6); do they understand that "their colleagues in the public schools now look for people who are highly knowledgeable in teacher education and who can articulate the process of becoming an effective teacher to those with whom they come in contact" (Marrou, 1988, p. 18); do they realize that accountability of the amount and quality of supervisory assistance is a priority in many school-university partnerships (Marrou, 1988); are they aware that student teaching is the single most important experience in the preservice teacher education program, that the supervisory role is very complex and demanding, and that not all "good" teachers and administrators can be effective university supervisors?

Knowledgeable, accountable, and effective university supervisors need preparation in certain knowledge bases and need to develop special attitudes, skills, and attributes. Knowledge bases in the philosophical, psychological, and sociological foundations of education are addressed in Chapters 4, 5, and 6. An overview of the attitudes, skills, experiences, and attributes, of well-prepared supervisors are addressed in the remainder of this chapter.

ATTITUDES

While there are many attitudes that effective supervisors possess, we address what we believe to be the five most important.

The first important attitude is *commitment*. If individuals have no real desire to work with student teachers and no desire to supervise, obviously they should not! Student teachers need and deserve dedicated individuals to help them through the most important and challenging time of their undergraduate careers.

This attitude of commitment is essential because it assures student teachers that supervisors will do all they can to provide a placement where student teachers feel accepted, trusted, and psychologically safe—one where they can be successful and realize their potential.

The second important attitude is *acceptance*. Student teachers can best feel accepted if they are listened to with understanding and if university supervisors clearly demonstrate that they care about what student teachers say, feel, and do.

The third attitude is *trust*. If an atmosphere of unconditional acceptance has been established during conferences and seminars, building a high level of trust can be accomplished. In such an environment, student teachers can risk the self-disclosure necessary for analyzing their self-perceptions.

The last important attitude of university supervisors is one of *giving*, especially the giving of positive feedback. A supervisor's praise can inspire, encourage, make others feel worthwhile, and create a positive climate (Major, 1984).

EXPERIENCES

A second important qualification of well-prepared supervisors is experience—experience as a classroom teacher, as an intern, as a student studying in a course on how to supervise.

Most university supervisors are required to have at least three years of successful classroom teaching experience at the appropriate elementary or secondary levels. This is a sound practice because teaching helps supervisors understand what it takes to be a full-time teacher: the ability to work with colleagues, cooperate with parents, discipline children, take attendance, collect lunch money, chaperone a dance, supervise the lunchroom, plan, instruct, evaluate, budget, and on and on. Remembering these activities can create empathy for student teachers.

A second experience that new supervisors need is an internship. The internship is as valuable to the preparation of the university supervisor as student teaching is to the education major and as the residency is to the medical student. Novice supervisors can learn much from veterans who have successfully supervised/taught. Veterans understand philosophies of the communities in which student teachers teach and know which schools and cooperating teachers provide excellent experiences.

Veterans also know how and when to respond to student teachers' comments. For example, early in the term, should a student teacher say, "My cooperating teacher and I do not agree on anything! Can you *please* put me in another school?" veterans will not panic and immediately locate a new assignment. Veteran supervisors know that personality conflicts between student teachers and cooperating teachers are rare and that student teachers are seldom reassigned based upon their own assessment of the relationship so early in the term. University supervisors would make it clear to the student teacher that although personality conflicts occur, that in itself is not grounds for moving to a new assignment.

Patterning the clinical experience model, the novice observes the veteran at work and vice versa. Periodic conferences are held so that novices can, among other things, reflect, analyze, learn about themselves, and ask questions.

A third experience, especially for university supervisors who have no formal preparation in supervision, is a course on the "Supervision of Student Teaching." Such a course is taught by successful veteran supervisors. As with the internship, novices can gain new perspectives on supervision from veterans.

The following topics might be considered for discussion in a course on the "Supervision of Student Teaching": public rela-

tions and effective communication; how to observe and evaluate
student teachers; how to conduct effective conferences and seminars; how to work with first-time cooperating teachers; strategies for interviewing, placing, and orienting student teachers;
roles and responsibilities of cooperating teachers; adult learning
theory; how university/college policy affects the student teaching
program; an update on research in teacher education; and leadership skills for training cooperating teachers.

Professional development experiences such as an internship
or a course in supervision allow new teacher educators to develop the skills and the self-confidence necessary to become
effective supervisors. Ideally, a novice supervisor would simultaneously serve as an intern and take a course as described
above.

SKILLS

A third qualification of university supervisors is the ability to
use special supervisory skills. While there are many skills required of effective supervisors—for example, observing, conducting conferences, facilitating seminars, counseling,
communicating, and evaluating—only positive communication
and the appropriate use of evaluation processes are addressed
in this section.

The skills of effective positive communication and appropriate
use of evaluation processes are necessary because university
supervisors need to maintain the delicate balance among the
student teachers' needs, the cooperating teachers' needs, and
the teacher education program goals. During each observation,
supervisors select and use appropriate observation, conference,
and evaluation strategies. They know when to give support and
praise and when to give constructive criticism.

Effective positive communication is an important skill because
university supervisors spend nearly all of their time communicating with K–12 administrators, cooperating teachers, student
teachers, and university personnel. Communication occurs
while placing student teachers, conferencing with cooperating
and student teachers, providing in-service, mediating between
K–12 school personnel and student teachers, and serving as a

liaison for the university. How supervisors communicate with all these people and in all these situations is extremely important to the success of the student teaching program.

No matter with whom you are communicating, "... the best most positive communication requires purpose, planning, and thoughtful execution" (Lang, Quick, & Johnson, 1981, p. 61). Positive communication is a two-way street. Both parties must listen and talk.

> Most college supervisors will testify that communication becomes far more positive between the two after it has become personalized; both parties listening and talking to each other, and both willing to accept the other's right to his position. Time has a rather amazing way of reconciling what would appear at first to be irreconcilable differences. (Lang, Quick, & Johnson, 1981, p. 53).

A specific way in which supervisors communicate with student and cooperating teachers occurs when cooperating teachers are reluctant to share negative feedback with student teachers (i.e., you should not take naps in the teachers' lounge or in the classroom; you should not chew gum while teaching; you need to be better groomed—wear socks, wear a tie, press your clothes, and use mouthwash and deodorant; and you are being perceived as arrogant and cocky by other teachers). University supervisors must diplomatically relay the cooperating teacher's concerns so that problems are solved yet maintain a good rapport within the triadic relationship.

Positive communication requires university supervisors to be open-minded and empathetic. While making decisions, university supervisors consider the best interests of the student teacher, the cooperating teacher, the cooperating school, and the teacher education program goals. Keeping persons with different ideas and perspectives content is not always an easy task but it is a necessary one!

Empathy is an equally important characteristic of positive communication. Being able to put yourself in the student teacher's position is essential if you are truly going to help this person grow and develop. We must understand the precarious position of student teachers. They are students, yet assume a teacher's responsibilities. They are expected to "take over" the classroom as if it is their own, yet it really belongs to another teacher. Individuals in a new situation are fragile and insecure; it is easy to hurt their feelings. The art of communication lies in telling student teachers what they need to hear, yet doing so in such a way that their feelings are not hurt and they become more secure.

A second major skill necessary for effective supervision is proper use of evaluation processes. University supervisors engage in the evaluation of student teachers in several ways. First, supervisors themselves select and use evaluation processes appropriate for each student teacher. Second, they tell cooperating teachers which processes are available for their use in evaluating student teachers. And third, they help cooperating teachers understand the university policy for assessing student teachers.

In conjunction with selecting appropriate evaluation processes (these will be addressed in detail in Chapter 8), supervisors are concerned with diagnostic, formative, and summative evaluation of student teachers.

When supervisors initiate the evaluation process, they realize that each student teacher begins at a different level of readiness. At the diagnostic level, variables such as personality, attitude, experience, achievement, and aptitude are considered (Borich, 1977). Thus, in fairness to each student teacher, university supervisors must be objective in their observations and evaluation and not compare one student teacher to another. Rather, they measure each student's growth from the last visit to the present.

Throughout the term, supervisors are continually assessing (formative evaluation) student teachers. The feedback they give is critical to student teachers' professional growth. Feedback helps to:

> . . . identify those things that we are doing right and those things that need improvement, what is working and what is not. Thus, the evaluation process is a mechanism for improvement, a process which helps us get closer to our objectives. It provides us with feedback which helps us to

make decisions about our objectives, strategies and activities. (Gay, 1980, p. 12)

In working with cooperating teachers throughout the term, university supervisors "interpret the evaluation procedure, the philosophy, objectives and importance of evaluation" (Lang, Quick, & Johnson, 1981, p. 141). Such an interpretation may include an explanation of evaluation processes, conferencing techniques, self-evaluation, and pupil evaluation of the teacher, as well as techniques of observation such as the use of rating scales, checklists, analysis forms, and the use of audio and video recorders. These and other techniques of observation and evaluation processes are elaborated upon in Chapters 7 and 8.

At the end of the term, university supervisors write a final (summative) evaluation of each student teacher. These evaluations become a part of students' permanent credential files. Supervisors need to remember "the student teacher is the direct responsibility of the college . . . and must be protected from unjust evalutaion" (Lang, Quick, & Johnson, 1981, p. 141). Needless to say, this evaluation should be written with great care. Supervisors also need to guard against those within the university who would, during the last and most important term of a student's undergraduate career, shirk the responsibility of evaluation entirely by shifting it solely from the degree-granting institution onto the cooperating teacher and school.

ATTRIBUTES

Attributes of high-quality university supervisors include: being conscientious, caring, empathetic, open-minded, tactful, and adaptable to many situations; and, having a good sense of humor, a positive problem-solving attitude, and a healthy self-esteem (Marrou, 1988).

In summary, there is a documented need for well-prepared university supervisors. Supervisors need special attributes and attitudes that allow them to demonstrate commitment, acceptance, openness, and trust; they need appropriate teaching, internship, and course experiences; and, among other skills, they need to be able to utilize effective positive communication and evaluation processes. Well-prepared, skillful, and giving university supervisors are needed as much as well-prepared, skillful, and giving teachers. It takes a special person, a skillful person, to effectively manage successful experiences for student teachers.

Chapter 4 _____

Preparation of the University Supervisor: Philosophical Foundations

We make intelligent and sound educational decisions only when we understand our own personal beliefs about education and teaching and only when we know how knowledge of the foundation areas of philosophy, psychology, and sociology will influence the decisions we make as supervisors. This chapter addresses the area of philosophy.

A philosophy is an individual's beliefs about the general principles of a field of knowledge—in this case, the field of teaching and learning. Developing an educational philosophy is a slow and intimate process because it is the sum of our attitudes, beliefs and experiences acquired over the years. A philosophy guides everything we do from how we teach to how we plan to how we interact. That is why it is so important for university supervisors to understand their philosophy. It prevents them from mindlessly going about their very important task. Understanding the different philosophies of education is also key to understanding the teaching practices and beliefs of each cooperating and student teacher.

Major differences between the basic philosophies of idealism, realism, scholasticism, classical humanism, experimentalism, and existentialism are described in very readable texts such as

Existential Encounters for Teachers by Maxine Greene (1967), *Historical and Contemporary Philosophies of Education* by Frederick C. Gruber (1973), *Introduction to the Philosophy of Education* by George F. Kneller (1964), *Issues and Alternatives in Educational Philosophy* by George R. Knight (1982), *Existentialism in Education: What It Means* by Van Cleve Morris (1966), and *Existential Philosophers: Kierkegaard to Merleau-Ponty* edited by George A. Schrader (1967).

Educational theories based upon these philosophies include essentialism, behaviorism, perennialism, progressivism, reconstructionism, futurism, existentialism, and humanism. The majority of American public schools, however, reflect essentialist, progressive, existentialist, and humanistic ideals. Therefore, only these four educational theories will be addressed.

ESSENTIALISM

Essentialism is rooted in idealism and realism. Initially, essentialists were one of several groups of critics who reacted against the principles of progressivism. Early essentialists such as William C. Bagley and Isaac L. Kandel argued for the need to emphasize "essentials," that is, the three R's.

Their works were followed by the writings of Mortimer Smith, Arthur Bestor, James Conant, and Max Rafferty. These writings, as well as the launching of Sputnik I in 1957, sustained essentialism in education in the 1950s and 1960s. Pleas from concerned citizens to go back to the basics nourished this philosophy into the 1970s and 1980s.

Some general characteristics of an essentialist program include: (1) emphasizing a subject matter curriculum (2) making the teacher the person in command—the one who decides what is to be taught, how it is to be taught, and when it is to be taught (3) holding scholarship as the key to successful students and programs (4) emphasizing memorization and drill (5) preparing students to function in society and (6) placing less emphasis upon the interests and desires of the student. Since so much emphasis is placed upon the core subjects of English, mathematics, and science, critics argue that an elitist mentality prevails in such schools, and that the haves and have-nots are sorted much too early in life.

PROGRESSIVISM

"Progressivism in education was part of a larger sociopolitical movement of general reform that characterized American life in the late nineteenth and early twentieth centuries" (Knight, 1982, p. 80). Educators such as John Dewey, William H. Kilpatrick, George S. Counts, and Boyd H. Bode greatly influenced the progressive movement in education during this period.

A school that reflects a progressive philosophy counters the ideas of "traditional education" and has some of the following characteristics: (1) active as opposed to passive children (2) a child-centered curriculum (3) a teacher who serves as a guide and facilitator of learning (4) problem-solving and project-oriented activities (5) a democratic, shared decision-making process (6) the premise that education *is* life and (7) the teaching of self-discipline. Since less emphasis is placed upon the role of authority figures in the classroom and within the program, critics argue that progressive programs are lax.

EXISTENTIALISM

Søren Kierkegaard, the Danish theologian of the early 1800s, was the first major existential thinker. Others include Friedrich Nietzsche, Martin Heidegger, Karl Jaspers, Gabriel Marcel, Albert Camus, Jean-Paul Sartre, Paul Tillich, and Rollo May.

Existentialists urge us to be aware of self, of freedom, of choice, of responsibility, and of authenticity. They believe that we are the authors of our own lives and can choose any goal. Except for being born, they assert, we make all decisions and are in charge of everything that happens in our lives. They ask us to ponder why we have been born and to understand that only through accepting death as the most important event in life we can sort the essential from the trivial and become truly aware of the values in life. They encourage us to examine our life and ask if we are living it to the fullest or if we are just existing.

Existentialists want people to live in such a way that their lives make a statement about what a human being ought to be. They want it to have mattered that we lived at all. They believe that values are very personal and can change, and that we should be ourselves rather than a stereotype of a group. Unpopularity, they believe, should never be feared because often its opposite, popularity, can only be purchased at the price of losing our integrity. Humans, they assert, must be taught to have courage and independence, for it is much easier to fear freedom and live by directions, sanctions, and ethical principles handed down from on high than it is to be aware that every word and every deed is a choice and that we must decide what to believe and what propositions are meaningful and significant. Existentialists believe that all of life is ad-lib, that we are given a script with blank pages, and that we become what we conceive ourselves to be. They believe that either we make ourselves or allow others to decide how we should live our only life.

If an existentialist were to overhear someone say, "I had to do what I did; I had no alternative," the existentialist would reply, "You have forfeited *your* freedom. *You* do not know *you* are human."

They believe that even those who consent to convention and conformity can be authentic *if* they are aware of this act of consenting and hence accept the responsibility for living their life in a conventional way.

Existentialists want people to know they are free, to know they have choices, to accept responsibility for their own behavior, to be in charge of their own lives, and to live without self-deception or self-delusion. They want human beings to rejoice in the fact that essence has not already been given, for if it had human beings would not be free. They want human beings to live their lives in such a way that it would be a tragedy if loss of life or annihilation were followed by obliteration and nothingness.

A school reflecting an existentialist philosophy provides occasions to intensify the students' decision-making awareness; it offers opportunities for students to work from the center of their private experiences, to generate personal meanings that the world may have for them; it lifts students over the crowd and helps them see that they are responsible for their desire to flee responsibility and cannot return to a state where no responsibility is demanded; and it helps make students aware of their own importance.

Teachers concentrate on asking questions to which they do not know the answer (i.e., "Why do we have a need for God?" "How can I matter in the scheme of things when the cosmos does not require my presence?").

They are against all methods that would put group thinking above the individual's thinking. They encourage students to realize that organizational affiliations take away as much as they offer. And they encourage students to ask, "So what?" when material is presented and to pursue such questions.

An existential teacher does not produce replicas but rather people who stand apart from themselves even more drastically than when they first met. Such a teacher believes that students are not things to be aligned into a predetermined notion of what they should be.

The curriculum focuses upon how life in the present might be lived and how we might solve problems. It is an attempt to help students find meaning in an apparently indifferent world and ask such questions as, "If the human race were to be turned to cinders, what would be the world's loss?" Knowledge is not an end in itself but a means toward self-development and self-fulfillment.

"Death," "love," "conflict," "pain," "suffering," "guilt," "freedom," and "joy" are addressed because they are always with us and by examining them now we may be allowed to meet them with more wisdom in the future. Teaching for happiness is exposed as a delusion, and idealistic beliefs are exposed as myths.

Existentialists scorn following the crowd and are against educating children at the same rate in the same way; they are against groups because students in groups gravitate toward the middle and a few dominate; they dislike parents giving over their control to the school for they believe the home is the greatest educative force; and they are against teachers imposing values and resist anyone who blames the environment, or the family, or the influence of another for their own fate.

If all learning activities were pursued in a mode and attitude similar to present-day extracurricular programs (i.e., the chess club, the school paper, the student council), they would be quite pleased.

Existentialists are often accused by fundamentalists of preaching the religion of secular humanism in the public schools.

HUMANISM

Educational humanism began in the 1950s as a reaction to an emphasis upon subject matter with little attention to effective education and as a part of the human potential movement in psychology. Humanistic psychologists such as Abraham Maslow, Arthur Combs, and Carl Rogers have focused their writings and works on helping the student, in their terms, become "self-actualized," become a "fully functioning person," and "fully develop one's self."

The push for attention to effective outcomes in education became strong in the 1960s when many writers and romantic critics of education flooded the market with books about the inhumane treatment of students and the jail-like structure of the public schools. Among these critics were writers such as Paul Goodman, John Holt, Herbert Kohl, and Jonathan Kozol.

Humanism in education has its roots in existentialism and progressivism. It stresses the uniqueness of each individual yet places emphasis upon the group. Humanistic approaches to teaching resemble a combination of individualized and small-group instruction. These approaches may include role playing, cross-age tutoring, sensitivity training, and affective exercises. Individuality is strongly expressed in the principles of humanistic education. Some of these principles include: (1) students learn what they want and need to know, (2) learning how to learn is more important than learning facts, (3) student self-evaluation is the only meaningful form of evaluation, (4) students' feelings are as important as facts, (5) learning to express one's emotions is as important as learning to think, and (6) learning occurs only in a nonthreatening environment.

Successful implementation of these humanistic principles requires a teacher who encourages, facilitates learning, gives guidance, trusts students, accepts students' feelings, utilizes student contracts with self-reporting techniques, and is more open, genuine, and a lifelong learner. In conclusion, most teachers have an eclectic philosophy. Few teachers have a philosophy of education associated with only one school of thought, yet they all have a point of view that guides them.

University supervisors work in many different public, private, and parochial schools. Each school community harbors its own purposes, aims, and beliefs in education. The educational philosophy that a cooperating teacher, administrator, school, district, or community holds should not concern the university supervisor. What should matter is that the supervisor be able to recognize these differences, maintain an open mind, and place the student teacher in a cooperating school that provides optimal growth in developing a personal philosophy of education. Placement in a school district different from the one in which the student teacher graduated from high school is often more beneficial than an assignment in a familiar school setting because we learn more from those who are different from ourselves. Student teachers need to understand how educational philosophies affect teaching styles. Too often they try to emulate their cooperating teachers, or cooperating teachers encourage them to teach the way their students have been used to learning. What works well for cooperating teachers may not necessarily work well for student teachers. During post-observation conferences, university supervisors can help student teachers think about what they are doing, why they are doing it, and how they can learn more from others' differences than from those who are similar.

Supervisors can help student teachers clarify their thoughts about planning, methodology, grading, discipline, physical arrangement of the room, rules, what they like about students and staff, and how to work more effectively with parents, peers, and fellow teachers. Such thinking will help them develop a personal philosophy of teaching.

Occasionally, university supervisors need to remind cooperating teachers how important it is for student teachers to develop a philosophy of education that will aid them in developing a personal teaching style. Cooperating teachers must be willing to allow student teachers to experiment with methodology. Without freedom to experiment, developing a personal philosophy of teaching is difficult if not impossible.

Chapter 5 ———————————————————————

Preparation of the University Supervisor: Psychological Foundations

This chapter is a synopsis of psychological principles that supervisors need to know. These principles are included under the following concepts: learning, learner characteristics, reinforcement, learning styles, punishment, motivation, and measurement and evaluation.

LEARNING

What do supervisors need to know about learning? They should know: the student's readiness to learn is contingent upon maturity, the ability to see how the learning experience affects him or her, the previous level of understanding, and expectation of success or failure; the ability to learn increases with age; the more we learn, the more we are capable of learning; the best time to learn is when the learning is useful; recall shortly after learning reduces the amount of learning forgotten, and; students "think" when they are given an intellectual challenge.

In *Retention Theory for Teachers*, Hunter (1967) states that retention may be increased through meaningfulness, degree of original learning, schedule of practice, feeling tone, and positive and negative transfer. Elaborating on feeling tone, she writes:

We remember the best those things that are associated with pleasant feeling tone. Next we remember those things that are associated with unpleasant feeling tones although we may try to eliminate them from memory by repressing them. We have a difficult time remembering those things that have no feeling tone associated with them. (p. 16)

In *Teach for Transfer*, Hunter (1971) says positive transfer occurs:

When other learnings in your past experiences help you learn and remember something in the present. The more similar learnings are, the more we get transfer from one to the other. To increase their transfer we teach the new by pointing out its similarity to the already learned. (p. 21)

[Negative transfer occurs] whenever the memory of one learning interferes with another. To avoid negative transfer, we do not teach certain things and we stress differences. (p. 27)

Supervisors also need to know about *learning how to learn*. Students who know how to learn: can transfer this ability to all learning situations; become less dependent upon a teacher; have a better self-concept; and view life more positively. The process of learning how to learn is highly dependent upon making the goal of learning how to learn clear to students and then by exposing them to a variety of styles selected for their effectiveness in particular situations (Cornett, 1983).

In the area of learning, supervisors need to know what left and right brain research says about learning and gender. For example, Cornett (1983), citing Epstein's gender differentiation findings, notes that:

Girls often develop a left-hemisphere specialization at an earlier age than do boys. Girls can handle a more sophisticated reading curriculum than boys, but with the proper amount of time and teaching, boys can become good readers. Girls have been found to be inferior in visual-spatial tasks, such as map, chart and graph reading. [And] girls have a major growth spurt between ages 10–12, demonstrated by head growth twice that of boys the same age (reflecting brain enlargement). (p. 23)

And finally, supervisors should realize that "attention to and motivation for tasks are complex internal states highly dependent on the learner's plans, intentions, and past experiences" (Cornett, 1983, p. 25). Because of this, teachers need to provide a rationale for goals, provide time for genuine reflection, give examples of relevancy while capitalizing on students' past experiences, and give students choices in selecting goals so that they can structure their own learning.

LEARNER CHARACTERISTICS

University supervisors should know that learners behave in ways representative of their ages, maturity levels, thinking abilities, social skills, and moral reasoning.

Children ages five to seven: need movement, noise, vigorous exercise, and active games with unrestrained running and jumping; want, need, and like to play in mud, walk in fallen leaves, and roll down hills; want to take part in simple group play; demand attention from the teacher; show off in front of playmates; quickly become engrossed in dramatic and rhythmic activities; have a short attention span; are easily fatigued (may withdraw from play); need training in habits of personal hygiene (covering coughs and sneezes, using handkerchiefs, keeping fingers away from mouth and nose); and need training in choice of clothing appropriate to weather.

Children ages eight to ten: have a wider range of interests and longer attention spans; need an assured social group position such as membership in a gang or secret club; like to set up their own standards and rules yet strongly desire understanding and sympathy from adults; need activities involving the whole body (stunts, throwing, running, and catching); demand consistency and individual justice; desire prestige and may seek it through boasting, rivalry, and calling attention to their size and strength; need to learn good fellowship and leadership; have a keen sense of rhythm; need organized games for team play; and gain self-confidence by excelling in one particular activity.

Children ages eleven to thirteen: grow very rapidly; may be uneasy and embarrassed about their body changes; become interested in the opposite sex and may express interest by showing off or even by excessive shyness and withdrawal; may be overanxious about health (good time to establish a balanced diet, teach first aid, and discuss group health problems); take more interest in personal appearance (good time to establish habits of cleanliness and grooming and to remedy poor posture); begin developing their own age codes; become less concerned about adult approval; become more interested in being with a few close friends; are willing to practice long and hard to gain skill in group games; need games requiring increased organization and firm rules, such as softball and soccer; need to develop spectatorship as well as sportsmanship; and (in the United States) may show interest in money-making activities.

Adolescents ages fourteen to sixteen: are nearing the end of the awkward age; are completing their puberty cycle; may have a period of glandular instability that causes them to burst with energy one day and feel let down the next; are reaching physiological adulthood but lack experience; exhibit a know-it-all attitude but inwardly may feel insecure; need guidance from teachers and parents; are quick to resent anything that impinges upon their feeling that they are adults; want a balance between security and freedom; are frequently overconfidant about what they can do and take on more than is good for their health; may develop a close attachment and admiration for some adult (this is a time of hero worship in fiction and in real life); like and want to attach themselves to a "worthy cause"; are grateful for a well-ordered, friendly, and warmhearted classroom atmosphere that provides a haven from the confusion of widened horizons; and may be self-conscious about sex (social dancing provides satisfying boy-girl relationships and is, therefore, a must for this age group).

Adolescents ages seventeen to nineteen: have a higher self-concept than younger adolescents; find psychological tasks such as role identity difficult without parental and peer support; are able to solve many of their problems if they have attained formal operational thought; do not make rational decisions about sexuality and drug use if they are cognitively immature; identify strongly with their generation; and, tend to become delinquent if they do not care about the values of their parents or society.

This specific information is helpful to student teachers who do not recognize what constitutes normal behavior for a given age group. Student teachers who expect sixth graders to sit still while listening to a lecture on rocks and minerals for forty minutes are being unrealistic. Student teachers who teach third graders like they teach senior high choirs are opening the door to frustration. And student teachers who expect seventh graders to behave the same as sophomores are likely to have problems.

University supervisors are in a position not only to help student teachers understand what is normal but to guide them toward using more appropriate expectations and methodology.

REINFORCEMENT

University supervisors need to know: reinforced behaviors are more likely to recur; reinforcement, to be most effective, must immediately follow the desired behavior; praise and external reinforcement have a positive effect on some students; improvement is contingent upon information about the success or lack of success of the effort; and, some learners need extrinsic rewards while others find satisfaction in the reward itself.

LEARNING STYLES

Research findings on style-based instruction indicate: teacher learning styles have an effect on teacher teaching styles; matching teaching methods to students' learning styles leads to higher achievement (Claxton & Murrell, 1987; Dunn, 1990); ability to learn is affected by environmental, emotional, sociological, and physical stimuli (Dunn & Dunn, 1978); and style matching improves students' self-concepts and increases satisfaction and mutual regard between teachers and students (Cornett, 1983; Dunn & Dunn, 1978; Dunn, 1990; Hand, 1990).

Collecting data on students' learning styles helps teachers identify those students who will not do well without special help. A learning styles approach works with potential dropouts (Perrin, 1990) and with mildly handicapped students (Brunner & Majewski, 1990).

Critics of style-based instruction contest several points, including (1) confusion about what exists regarding common definitions, (2) the weakness in reliability and validity of measurement, and (3) identification of relevant characteristics in learners and instructional settings (Curry, 1990, p. 50).

Others also report findings that contradict a learning styles approach. They charge that style matching produces inconsistent achievement outcomes (Cornett, 1983); that there is little evidence matching instruction to students' learning styles will raise scores (O'Neill, 1990); and that "learning style studies showing effects achieve the effects by aligning instruction, not by matching instruction and style" (Curry, 1990, p. 54).

The most controversial issue associated with learning style theory is the relationship between cultural backgrounds and learning style (O'Neill, 1990). For instance, Claxton and Murrell (1987), in describing findings on learning styles for Native American, Chicano, Japanese, and Vietnamese children, report:

> Many Native American children are primarily visually oriented and excel in visually related skills like penmanship, spelling and art. Thus they are at a disadvantage in typical classrooms where verbal skills, classroom discussions, and question-and-answer sessions are emphasized. They are more used to learning through observation, through practice that is carefully directed by an adult, and through imitation. They typically resist competition and emphasize cooperation in learning.
>
> Chicano children have been socialized in a culture that emphasizes cooperative and peer interaction rather than individualistic competition . . . and many . . . are motivated more by social reinforcement and by helping others.
>
> Studies of Japanese and Chinese children show they tend to be able to respond quickly and accurately on timed tests, although a study of Chinese children shows they prefer time for reflecting before answering.
>
> Vietnamese children are used to a traditional educational

system that emphasizes rote learning, memorization, repetition, and recollection. (p. 70)

Proponents argue that recognition of these differences in learning styles and application of appropriate strategies is vital to students' success. It is also important to note that cognitive styles vary as much within ethnic, racial, and socioeconomic status and groups as they do between groups (Shipman & Shipman, 1985).

Critics who are against the matching of teaching styles to cultural backgrounds believe this practice to be racist and discriminatory and geared to keeping a minority in their place (O'Neil, 1990). Researchers have developed many models to identify learning styles. Some of these include: Hill & Nunnery's (1973) *Cognitive Style Mapping*; Kagan's (1965) *Gregorc Style Indicator*; Canfield & Canfield's (1986) *Canfield Instrument Style Inventory*; Harvey et al. (1961) *Cognitive Complexity-Simplicity* model; Dunn, Dunn, & Price's (1975, 1989) *Learning Style Inventory*; Keefe & Monk's (1986) *Learning Style Profile*; Kolb's (1978) *Theory of Experiential Learning*; Mann et al. (1970) *Response Style model*; McCarthy's *(1972, 1990) 4MAT* model; McKenney & Keen's (1965) *Perceptive/ Receptive-Systematic/Intuitive* model; Myers & Briggs (1976) *Myers and Briggs Type Indicator*; and Witkin's (1976) *Field Dependent-Independent* model.

For additional information on learning style instruments, consult Cornett's (1983) monograph entitled *What You Should Know about Teaching and Learning Styles*. In a selected annotated bibliography, Cornett lists multidimensional as well as specific cognitive, affective, and perceptual modality instruments.

For the most recent information on learning styles and instruments, use "cognitive style," "perceptual style," "conceptual tempo," "encoding," "learning modalities," and "learning strategies" as descriptors.

PUNISHMENT

There is disagreement among experts about whether punishment is effective in changing old behaviors and in teaching new ones. There is good evidence that punishment can bring about changes in behavior, but there is no good evidence concerning the multiple effects on learners or how learners feel about themselves or the punishing adult. Not enough is known about punishment to use it well.

Supervisors should know specifically that: punishment of extreme intensity could suppress a behavior permanently; children learn to avoid situations that are likely to result in punishment; punishment causes anxiety; mild punishment may reduce the frequency of a behavior or it may simply reduce the frequency of a behavior in the presence of the punisher; and what is punishment for one individual may not be for another.

In writing about what teachers should know about punishment, Major (1990) states:

> We punish to prevent deviant behavior from the individual being punished; to sustain the morale of the conformist; to express to all that the school disapproves of the wrong being done; to neutralize the deviate as a role model; to protect other students; to make certain that everyone sees that those who do wrong cannot get ahead of those who do right; and we punish so that students will know a rule, not just a request. (p. 50)

MOTIVATION

University supervisors need to know: students learn more when they attempt tasks that are not too easy yet not too difficult; unmotivated students should be given very short assignments; motivation increases when the learner is genuinely involved; with increased motivation, students improve and go beyond the minimum requirements; and, maximum satisfaction and learning occur when students select and plan a project and set their own goals.

MEASUREMENT AND EVALUATION

University supervisors should be familiar with measurement and evaluation because they assist student teachers with these in several ways.

They examine lesson plans and look for appropriate and well-written objectives. They explain the pros and cons of using essay versus objective tests and criterion- and norm-referenced tests. And they help student teachers during seminars and conferences reflect upon teaching practices.

What advice about measurement and evaluation should supervisors give? First, they should tell student teachers that what they measure must be clearly related to what they are trying to teach. To ensure this, student teachers need to develop unit or lesson plans that include objectives/purposes, contents/concepts, methodology, materials, and plans for assessment. A lesson design, according to Hunter (1982), has eight critical attributes: anticipatory set, objectives/purposes, input, modeling, checking for understanding, guided practice, independent practice, and closure.

As mentioned earlier, the most crucial attribute of a lesson plan is the instructional objective that must precisely state what is to be learned. As Cooper (1977) points out:

There is considerable evidence to support the contention that when teachers have clearly defined instructional objectives and have shared them with their students, a number of things happen: 1) better instruction occurs, 2) more efficient learning results, 3) better evaluation occurs and 4) students become better self-evaluators. (p. 77)

Instructional objectives should also span the six levels of performance activity: knowledge; comprehension; application (ability to use abstractions, rules, principles, ideas, and methods); analysis (ability to break something down into its constituent parts); synthesis (ability to put elements together to form a whole); and evaluation (ability to draw conclusions and form opinions) (Bloom, 1956). Many teachers focus primarily upon the first three levels. University supervisors can encourage student teachers to develop objectives (and questioning techniques) at the analysis, synthesis, and evaluation levels to promote critical thinking, as all students are capable of functioning at these levels.

Second, supervisors should tell student teachers that measurement should be frequent enough so that random variables do not cause student teachers to make inaccurate judgments about their students' true abilities. They can also encourage student teachers to use a variety of testing procedures such as oral exams, teacher-made essay and objective tests, and standardized tests, as well as nontesting procedures such as rating scales, checklists, anecdotal records, and observation.

University supervisors need to be aware that student teachers are most concerned about measurement and evaluation when they need to construct essay and objective tests. Essay tests are powerful because of the technical capability of assessing students' thinking at any level in the cognitive domain. They are best used to assess thinking at higher levels (analysis, synthesis, and evaluation). The major weakness of an essay test is its susceptibility to unreliable scoring.

Objective tests include true-false, multiple choice, and matching questions. Each type has its own strengths and weaknesses. Major (1981) provides sound advice for constructing objective tests: "true-false statements should not include give-away words like *all, none,* and *never* for a question that is false or *occasionally, usually,* or *seldom* for a question that is true" (p. 9). Multiple choice questions should be written as follows: the stem should be written first, the correct answer second, and the distractors last; all distractors should be plausible; the correct answer should not always be the longest; and using answers like "all but *a* and *d*" should be avoided because overuse measures reading and rereading ability rather than what is intended (pp. 9–10). For matching tests, Major advises: put the exercise all on one page; logically order all responses and sets of items; include more responses than sets of items; and have sets contain no more than six or seven items (p. 9).

Overall, objective tests are flexible and capable of appraising recall of knowledge and more complex cognitive abilities. The major weakness, however, is that objective tests often evaluate only recall.

Third, university supervisors should encourage student teachers to help select the measurement instruments, either criterion- or norm-referenced, to be used in assessing students' performances. In their text *Educational Psychology,* Gage and Berliner

(1988) adapted the following information on criterion- and norm-referenced measurement from Clift and Imrie:

> Criterion-referenced measurement is useful for: evaluating individualized learning programs; estimating student ability in a particular area; measuring what a student has learned; certifying competency; controlling entry to successive units of instruction; and whenever mastery of a subject or skill is of prime concern.
> Norm-referenced measurements are useful for classifying students; selecting students for fixed quota requirements; and making decisions as to how much (more or less) a student has learned in comparison to others (pp. 578–579).

Student teachers learn about the differences between criterion- and norm-referenced measurement in foundations courses. Even so, university supervisors may need to assist them in the practical application of this knowledge to the classroom.

And finally, university supervisors can help student teachers in the area of measurement and evaluation by encouraging them to reflect upon their teaching practices and the decisions they make in the classroom. In addition, supervisors may help student teachers reflect upon the purposes and consequences of their actions as well as the constraints of the system in which they work. As Greene suggests:

> Neither the college nor the school can change social order, or legislate democracy; but something can be done to empower teachers to reflect upon their own life situations and speak out about what they deem to be decent, humane and just. (Zeichner & Liston, 1987)

This reflection may enable the development of self-directed growth and participation in educational policy making (Zeichner & Liston, 1987).

In summary, we hope that this brief review of learning, learner characteristics, learning styles, punishment, motivation, and measurement and evaluation will help university supervisors and encourage them to keep abreast of the psychological principles affecting teaching and learning.

Preparation of the University Supervisor: Sociological Foundations

Traditionally, courses like the Sociology of Education and the Sociology of Teaching have addressed such issues as social class, status, prestige, inequality, race relations, deviant behavior, and so on. It would be impossible for university supervisors to learn too much about these topics.

The existence of our pluralistic democratic society depends upon what future teachers learn about gangs; ways students look at life; discrimination; prejudice; effective communication skills; and how humans learn to use reason rather than force to resolve conflicts. University supervisors need to be lifelong learners in these areas.

Some citizens believe that the existence of our society is in jeopardy. They say things have changed for the worse, since 1964, when Malcolm X wrote "Most white men's hearts and guts will turn over inside of them, whatever they may have you otherwise believe, whenever they see a Negro man on close terms with a white woman" (Haley & Malcolm X, 1964). They challenge us to ask any person of color if their life has gotten better during the past ten years and if ignorance and racism are still alive in the United States.

In addition, these citizens point out that people in New York get killed for their three-quarter-length shearling leather coats ("New Crime," 1990); that unconscious, dying patients in hospitals have their wedding bands stolen from their fingers (Greene, 1991); that metal detectors are used every day at many high schools (Shanahan, 1990); that young persons are crushed and trampled to death at concerts (Greene, 1991); that 221 juveniles per 100,000 are in custody now, representing nearly a 20 percent increase during the past five years (Allen-Hagen, 1991); that "black murder is becoming acceptable, unalarming, even among blacks" (Jackson, 1990); and that, in spite of early parole, plea bargaining, lenient sentencing, and house arrest, jail and prison populations continue to set records year after year, and on a given day over 1 million people are incarcerated (National Institute of Justice Report, 1990). Read any newspaper, any day, they urge, and then ask yourself if our society *is* becoming more bizarre and less restricted each year.

As a baseline, in the area of sociological foundations, university supervisors need to help student teachers realize:

- by the year 2010 the Hispanic and Black populations will be equal in size, and 38 percent of our nation's citizens will be minority persons (Hodgkinson, 1990).

- that family—defined as a married couple with children under age eighteen—accounted for only 26 percent of America's 93.3 million households last year ("Decline of 'Traditional' Families," 1991).

- that more than 600,000 people immigrate to this country annually, and that in New York City, for example, one child in four under the age of ten is the offspring of a non-English-speaking immigrant parent (Sobol, 1990).

- that many Black students perform poorly in high school simply because they believe that academic success is a sellout to the white world.

University supervisors also need to help student teachers become aware:

- that schools must help students fight their feelings of powerlessness by developing within them a sense that they can make a difference in the world (Berman, 1990).

- that 14 percent of our nation's children are illegitimate, 15 percent have physical or mental handicaps, and 25 percent live in single-parent families (*Today's Education, 1987*).
- that of these single-parent families, many are what Ellen Goodman of the *Washington Post* calls "intact single-parent families." They are not broken, they are not on crutches, they are not "children of divorce," but rather they are children who have two parents who are no longer living together (Goodman, 1988).
- that most seniors have a preference for passive learning because nearly two-thirds of them work during the school year, and many work full-time or nearly full-time (Smart, 1986; "Teens Who Work," 1990).
- that 60 percent of our students say that teachers never ask them to relate their outside jobs to school work (Wisconsin Center for Educational Research News, 1984).

In addition, university supervisors need to remind student teachers:

- that many in the community of color look at the government in an adversarial way and believe, through every experience they have had, that the system is not sensitive to cultural diversity and there will be more violence in the future.;
- that students are not just imagining standardization is replacing pluralism. It is. Go to any town in America and see what people watch on TV, where they shop, where they eat, and what they wear—it is much the same.

University supervisors also need to remind student teachers:

- that students need to be taught the ideal of equality and how to function in roles they may not now believe are open to them.
- that although mobility is an essential goal of education, students need to learn that there is limited room at the top and only the most able and ambitious can reach it.
- that the high school completion rate for Hispanics, ages eighteen to twenty-four, was 55.9 percent in 1989 ("Rising Hispanic Dropout," 1991) and that by the year 2015, Hispanics will be the nation's largest minority.
- that while 62 percent of the single-parent families live below the

poverty level (*Today's Education*, 1987), and that one in eight youngsters in America under the age of twelve is hungry ("Study Finds 1 in 8," 1991), the majority of those who live in poverty are not able-bodied loafers. Many work full-time, but by being paid only minimum wage, they still cannot climb above the government-designated level of poverty. Some, through no fault of their own, find only part-time work with no health, vacation, or retirement benefits, and others are just too old, too young, or too physically handicapped to work.

And finally, university supervisors also need to help student teachers understand:

- that gangs survive because they provide support, a sense of belonging, safety, glamor, power, and an opportunity to once again dream and feel like "somebody."

- that trouble comes for many students at about the time they start getting "cut" from sports and plays and yet are still too young to drive or work.

- and that a commission, established by the *American Medical Association* and the *National Association of State Boards of Education*, reported, "On an average day . . . 135,000 students bring guns to school. Every year 1 million teenage girls, almost a tenth of the age group, become pregnant and 2.5 million adolescents contract a sexually transmitted disease. More than 1 million are regular users of drugs and alcohol-related accidents are the leading cause of death among teenagers" (Lewis, 1990).

You have gained a wealth of knowledge, experience, and expertise in the educational realm. Share your insights with student teachers so that they may become better observers of people, more tolerant and understanding of those from different backgrounds, and may inspire their students to better understand themselves and the society they will inherit. Fortunately, we are surrounded by easily accessible materials from which to learn.

Chapter 7

Observing Student Teachers

This chapter focuses on what university supervisors need to know prior to observing student teachers, what they need to look for while observing, and some specific techniques for making observations meaningful. Supervisors should remind themselves that each student teacher has a separate personal and academic background, motivational level, personality, intellectual capacity, and level of readiness that differs from his or her peers. The amount of formal clinical, volunteer, and work experiences with youth also varies.

Some student teachers have grown up in low socioeconomic but supportive environments and have a 3.7 grade-point average while others from upper-middle-income families have a 2.5 grade-point average. Some have had a goal of teaching since the first grade while others are in education because their parents want them to have job accessibility upon graduation. Some may be open and have an instant rapport with students and staff while others may be reserved, shy, and take more time to develop relationships. A few, from the beginning, understand what it takes to be a teacher while others need a lot of coaching. Some may prepare brilliant lessons while others struggle. Occasionally, student teachers are ready to teach a class the first or second day while others need a more gradual transition before accepting classroom responsibilities. Student teachers, like anyone else in a new situation, experience problems. They need kindness and support to make student teaching successful and productive.

Before observing, it is also important to make sure that student teachers are aware of your expectations, are aware of what will occur during your visits, and are aware of the techniques of observation you will use. A good time to share these expectations and techniques is during the first seminar before student teaching begins.

GENERAL TECHNIQUES

Tell student teachers whether your visits will be announced or unannounced, how many observations you plan to make, how much time you will spend observing during each visit, and what you will specifically look for while observing. Give them a copy of any forms you use. This process relieves much of the stress and anxiety caused by your visits. It also helps to organize your visits and makes each meaningful.

The most meaningful observations have a specific purpose and are preplanned and organized. If it is at all possible, schedule a pre-observation conference with the student teacher. During this conference, discuss the lesson to be taught (observed) and any teaching competencies and personal qualities that you or the student teacher want to focus on. This process ensures that more attention will be given to improving specific teaching competencies and personal qualities, thereby focusing less on generalities.

What does the university supervisor look for during an observation? Whether the observer is a generalist or subject-area specialist will dictate what is observed. The generalist observes professional competencies such as: planning; selection and organization of materials; creativity and innovation in classroom instruction; effectiveness of teaching procedures; provision for individual differences in student backgrounds; interests and abilities; use of available instructional resources; knowledge of subject matter; use of testing and evaluation techniques; and maintenance of discipline and morale.

More specifically, a generalist may observe and ask some of the following questions: Did the student teacher establish a positive set at the beginning of the lesson? Did the student teacher and students work toward a goal(s)? Were a variety of questions skillfully used (recalling facts, drawing inferences, vocabulary, and experience)? Did the student teacher capitalize on students' questions and give attention to their thoughts and ideas? Was the duration of the lesson appropriate for the subject matter and for the level of students being taught? Was the student teacher able to gain the attention and participation of most of the students in the class?

The generalist also observes personal qualities such as: relationships with fellow teachers; acceptance of criticism and suggestions; emotional maturity; ability to communicate orally; effectiveness of written communication; appropriateness of dress and personal grooming; physical vitality and alertness; initiative and resourcefulness; and professional interest and commitment to teaching.

Subject-area specialists observe some of what has been mentioned above, but they are also able to judge whether the student teacher has sufficient subject matter competence. Generalists, too, have their own area of expertise and are able to critique student teachers' competence in their respective fields.

It is helpful to both generalists and specialists to be aware of the student teacher's stage of development during each observation. Bennie (1972) describes a study that demonstrated five stages of gradual growth from concern about self to concern for students. The stages through which student teachers pass are: (1) concern for themselves (2) concern over their adequacy as teachers (3) concern with the causes of student behavior (4) concern involving what others thought of their teaching and (5) genuine concern over students and effectiveness of teaching (pp. 59–63).

While observing early in the term, university supervisors should also realize that the student teachers may just be surviving, first as people, second as teachers. They may not be ready to be observed. If this is the case, observations have no meaning for them. Time may be better spent in helping student teachers develop coping and management skills.

What techniques of observation do university supervisors use? They may observe and communicate formally or informally using verbal or nonverbal communication. They may also utilize one or more of the following specific techniques: anecdotal recording, numeric tallying, rating scales, checklists, split-half techniques, analysis systems, and video and audio recorders (these will be discussed in depth later in the chapter).

Supervisors who observe and communicate in a formal way schedule a pre-observation conference, an observation period, and a post-observation conference. They have met previously with student teachers to discuss expectations and techniques of observation to be used in each phase of the visit. They give a schedule of "announced" visits to each student and cooperating teacher. Such a schedule lists exact dates when supervisors are to visit a cooperating school. They arrange a visit to each student teacher approximately every ten days. They may also call student teachers the day before to confirm a visit.

A formal pre-observation conference makes the observation period more meaningful for the student teacher and university supervisor. It helps supervisors understand students' situations. Student teachers can share the objectives, methodology, and so on, of the lesson that the supervisors will observe; past and future circumstances that relate to the lesson or students; and, those areas in which they feel they have grown or need improvement. Student teachers may also ask university supervisors to observe a specific skill: for example, questioning techniques that they have been trying to improve on. Discussing such matters with student teachers in a pre-observation conference promotes a better understanding of what actually transpires in the classroom as supervisors make observations.

University supervisors who observe in a formal way also arrange a conference with the cooperating teacher. Discussion between the two serves as an update on the student teacher's progress from both of their perspectives. Cooperating teachers may ask supervisors to observe a particular aspect of the student teacher's performance, for example, to listen for ways in which the student teacher "talks down" to students. Student teachers can change how they talk to students if the supervisor and co-operating teacher both observe this unintentional approach and both make suggestions for improvement. At times, the observation and suggestions made by two professionals more strongly reinforces the change of a particular behavior. The observation period is made more meaningful for the supervisor and student teacher, because the cooperating teacher has had an opportunity to confer with the university supervisor. The supervisor may observe something that the cooperating teacher has missed. He or she then shares this observation with the cooperating teacher during a post-observation conference.

During a formal post-observation conference with a student teacher, the university supervisor discusses and shares any written comments or forms. A copy of these comments or forms can be given to the student teacher and kept in a journal so that they are readily available for periodic self-analysis. While sharing feedback, "capitalize on a student teacher's strengths in such a way that the student will be aware of the situations in which his best points become most useful" (Nelson & McDonald, 1958, p. 32). Constructive criticism is successful only insofar as the student teacher accepts and endorses the observations (Bennie, 1972). Supervisors may tactfully try to help student teachers understand that "it is much better to accept unwarranted criticism, with the idea of making improvements, than to disregard such comments through a process of rationalization and perhaps, lose the value that you might otherwise receive" (Devor, 1964, p. 204). A mutual analysis of the student teacher's successes and failures and the causes of each helps the student strive for improvement (Bennie, 1972).

Supervisors who observe and communicate in an informal way may not schedule pre- and post-observation conferences. Their visits may be unannounced. They may not observe student teachers for a full class period. They may not use any special forms for observing teaching skills or personal qualities. And they may not leave any written comments with the student teacher. Even so, university supervisors who observe and communicate informally *do* make contact with both the student and cooperating teacher.

During an "informal" visit, there is an exchange of brief comments and suggestions among the triad. Informal observations can be as meaningful as formal ones. However, many aspects of student teaching and specific problems cannot be dealt with adequately during such a visit. Veteran supervisors use their expertise, judgment, and commonsense to determine whether and when the visit and observation should be formal or informal.

We caution novice supervisors to refrain from overusing informal observation techniques for two reasons. First is the issue of credibility. It takes years to build trust with cooperating teachers, administrators, and other K–12 personnel. It also takes time to establish a credible reputation with student teachers. Second is the issue of accountability. While cooperating school personnel have always held the university accountable in the student teaching partnership, in the past few years we have experienced a demand for even greater accountability. And student teachers are now paying high tuition for university services—namely, supervision. Novices may consider spending as much time as they can formally observing and communicating with student and cooperating teachers to build trust, credibility, and accountability. The veteran supervising in a new geographic region may also consider doing the same.

Whether university supervisors use formal or informal observation, nonverbal communication must not be ignored. Nonverbal behavior cues such as facial expressions, eye movements, gestures, posture, and body movements of the student and cooperating teacher tell the supervisor how they feel. The student and cooperating teacher are just as quick to interpret the university supervisor's nonverbal cues. A word of caution to the novice: be aware of how your nonverbal communication is perceived by the student teacher as you sit and observe from the back of the classroom. The student teachers' interpretation may affect how they conduct class.

Formal and informal observation techniques usually dictate whether the visits are announced or unannounced. Each type has advantages and disadvantages. Announced visits have several advantages. First, since the student and cooperating teachers know when the university supervisor will be observing, they can prepare a "model" lesson that demonstrates the skills and progress of the student teacher. This keeps the student teacher from using the crutch, "If only you had been here yesterday." Second, both the student and cooperating teachers can plan what they wish to discuss with the supervisor during the scheduled pre- and post-observation conferences. Third, and perhaps most important, is that the observation period becomes just that—a time when the supervisor observes, not evaluates, the student teacher. It is the supervisor's responsibility to establish an atmosphere conducive to observation rather than evaluation. A disadvantage of announced visits is that you never get to observe student teachers on a day when they are not "prepared."

Unannounced visits have the advantage of observing student teachers on any given day or class period. This may keep student teachers prepared and doing their best at all times since they do not know when to expect the university supervisor. On the other hand, supervisors may drop in on a day when the student teachers' classes are attending a lyceum, and they miss an opportunity to observe them. Another disadvantage of unannounced visits is that additional stress is often experienced by student teachers (who are already in a very stressful situation) because they are wondering when the supervisor will be stopping by.

Student teachers who have a problem and do not know when their supervisor is coming to see them may phone the supervisor at home. On the other hand, if student teachers know that the supervisor will be visiting in a day or two, they will most likely think the problem through rationally, be ready to share it with the supervisor during the scheduled observation, or have it solved by the time of the visit. Still another disadvantage of unannounced visits is that student teachers are likely to equate the visit with "evaluation" rather than observation.

Although the triad understands that evaluation is an ongoing process, the purpose of observations is to monitor growth and modify instructional behavior. The actual observation period is one in which the supervisor observes specifics, such as whether the student teacher taught the objective(s) of the lesson, called on as many girls as boys, asked higher-order questions, said "OK" only five times, and so on. The emphasis of an observation is on what was observed, improvements and areas in which the student teacher needs additional work. If student teachers understand that supervisors are there to help them improve as a teacher and not just to "evaluate," a nonthreatening and positive environment is more likely to be established, and student teachers will experience less stress.

SPECIFIC TECHNIQUES

There are many specific techniques that supervisors can use to observe student teachers. Our list is not all-inclusive. We describe those techniques that are used most often. No matter which techniques you use, the best advice we can offer is to be objective in your observations and accurately record behavior.

Anecdotal Recordings

One specific technique is to use anecdotal recordings, which are simply nearly word-for-word transcriptions of observations (some use Madeline Hunter's term "script taping"). University supervisors know that what goes on in the classroom is very complex, and it is difficult to observe everything. Therefore, anecdotal recordings are best used for only parts of the observation. Two advantages of this technique are that it is complete enough to be meaningful at a later date, and a collection of recordings can help in the interpretation of the student teacher's growth (Lang, Quick, & Johnson, 1981).

Numeric Tallying

Numeric tallying is a technique in which a particular behavior is inventoried. A few examples of how a supervisor might use numeric tallying are: counting the number of times a student teacher uses the word "OK" or says "ah" in pausing between thoughts; marking on a diagram of the classroom where the student teacher is positioned in relation to the students every five minutes; tallying the number of students that appear to be on or off task or the number of students who asked or answered questions; or noting on a diagram of the classroom which students talk and how frequently they talk. Numeric tallying provides only facts. It does not give explanations or comparisons of the observation with others' judgment of the situation.

Rating Scales

Rating scales are designed to monitor the level of performance of teaching competencies and personal qualities. Such scales are usually Likert-type scales. For example, each competency and quality listed on the scale may be followed by a numeric rating of 1 (low) to 5 (high) or a ranking of poor to excellent. The observer marks a number or ranking corresponding to his or her perception of the student teacher's level of proficiency. Rating scales cover a broad range of teaching skills and personal qualities. It is impossible to observe all the skills and qualities of the student teacher, however, frequent use of rating scales can show the student teacher's progress.

Checklists

Checklists are similar to rating scales in that they monitor the student teacher's level of performance but to a lesser extent. Unlike rating scales, checklists often consist of two or three categories, that is, whether the skill was observed or whether the skill was above the expected level, at the expected level, or requires more emphasis. Checklists provide student teachers with information in a general way. This information at a minimum is helpful without additional explanations by the observer.

Split-half Technique

Split-half technique is a method of observation whereby the supervisor records on one half of a sheet of paper specific observations or asks questions about something that happened or why something was done. The blank half sheet opposite the supervisor's recordings is reserved for the student teacher's response. This technique works well if it is used frequently, at a minimum once a week. Used in this way, it serves as a continuous dialogue between the student teacher and observer. The split-half technique also provides time outside the post-observation conference for student teachers to think about their responses. Its main disadvantage is that since the recordings tend to be randomized and are subjective, they focus only on specific happenings and ignore the more general and global view of what transpired during the period observed (Lang, Quick, & Johnson, 1981).

Analysis Systems

Analysis systems are techniques of observation focusing on factors such as teacher behavior and verbal interaction between the teacher and students or subject matter or instructional methods or personality characteristics (Lang, Quick, & Johnson, 1981).

Perhaps the most widely used interaction analysis system continues to be *Flanders' System of Interaction Analysis* (1971) as described in *The Role of the Teacher in the Classroom: A Manual for Understanding and Improving Teacher Classroom Behavior*. This system is used as a research tool and in-service training device for teachers. The supervisor is cautioned to receive training in the system before using it with student teachers (Lang, Quick, & Johnson, 1981).

Subject Matter Analysis Instruments and Techniques

Subject matter analysis instruments and techniques are intended to record the content proficiency of the student teacher. The few available instruments enable the observer to focus on the nature of the subject matter, not on how the student teacher makes use of it. Some professional organizations in fields such as English (National Council of Teachers of English), mathematics (National Council of Teachers of Mathematics), social studies (National Council for the Social Studies), and so on, have developed analysis scales or instruments. The university supervisor may want to contact these organizations for additional information.

Instructional Methods Analysis Instruments and Techniques

Instructional methods analysis instruments and techniques are observations designed to examine how well student teachers utilize and implement the appropriate methods. A major problem with this technique is that what constitutes an appropriate method is not agreed upon (Lang, Quick, & Johnson, 1981). Elaborating on this problem, Lang, Quick, and Johnson (1981) cite Sandefur and Bressler (1971) who wrote:

The paradox of classroom observation systems is that, while the profession now has the tools for qualifying teaching behavior, there are no generally accepted criteria for what constitutes effective teaching behavior. [Supervisors should not] evade or compromise methods oriented observations because of a lack of definition. (p. 108)

Lang and colleagues direct supervisors to consult Smith and Meux's (1962) *Study of the Logic of Teaching*, Simon and Boyer's (1970) *Mirrors for Behavior II: An Anthology of Observation Instruments*, and the *ATE Research Bulletin # 10* (1971) for information about specific observations of instructional methods.

Personality Characteristics Analysis Instruments and Techniques

Personality characteristics analysis instruments and techniques are tools to observe the teacher's personality and how it affects classroom climate and the extent to which students learn. The problem with this technique is not one of whether it is legitimate to observe personality but rather which personality characteristics most directly influence learning. Some personality characteristics that make a difference in how and whether students learn are: "being positive, liking young people, caring for individuals' rights and opinions, and openness" (Lang, Quick, & Johnson, 1981, p. 111). There are limited available instruments. Again, Lang and colleagues direct the supervisor to three sources for more information: *Mirrors of Behavior*, the *ATE*

Research Bulletin #10, and ASCD's (1969) *Improving Educational Assessment and An Inventory of Measures of Affective Behavior.*

Videocassette Recorder

The videocassette recorder is yet another observational tool. Studies citing use of the videocassette recorder as a tool for providing teaching effectiveness feedback to student teachers increased during the 1960s and declined steadily during the 1970s and 1980s.

The authors were interested in quantifying the extent to which videotaping currently is used as an instrument to help student teachers improve their teaching skills and in assessing the local accessibility of videotaping equipment to teachers and student teachers. A questionnaire about the use of the videocassette recorder was sent to 300 cooperating teachers within a sixty-mile radius of Mankato State University in southern Minnesota during the winter and spring quarters of 1990. A total of 229 (76 percent) responses were returned. Four questions about videocassette recording usage were asked. These questions and the number and percentage of responses are given below in the table entitled, "The VCR and Student Teachers."

1. Does your school have a videocassette recorder that you can access?

        YES   225   (98.3%)   NO   4   (1.7%)

2. Have you videotaped yourself in the past year?

        YES   70   (30.6%)   NO   159   (69.4%)

3. Have you videotaped your student teacher teaching a class?

        YES   77   (33.6%)   NO   152   (66.4%)

4. Do you have any suggestions concerning the use of videotaping for self-evaluation purposes? If so, please list them.

No formal statistical analysis of this data was calculated. Yet a quick glance at the percentages indicates that (1) the majority (98.3 percent) of cooperating teachers presently have access to videocassette recorders (2) less than one-third (30.6 percent) of the cooperating teachers have videotaped themselves in the past year and (3) one-third (33.6 percent) of the cooperating teachers videotaped their student teachers. All of the cooperating teachers who indicated that they taped themselves also indicated that they taped their student teachers. In answer to question four, many cooperating teachers noted that videotaping the student teacher was a good idea and they planned to videotape future student teachers. Also, a few cooperating teachers indicated that they would tape themselves in the near future.

"Videotaping alone will neither do the supervising nor improve instruction. However, properly utilized it can be a valuable tool" (Meierdiercks, 1981, p. 41). Research indicates that teachers who view their work and participate in developing suggestions for improving it are more successful in making appropriate changes (Allen, 1970; Franck & Samaniego, 1981).

A major advantage of videotaping is it provides immediate feedback to student teachers in analyzing their teaching effectiveness, that is, voice and speech patterns, use of praise, variety of questions asked, clarity of directions, elicitation of class participation, classroom climate, and many other factors of effectiveness. The videocassette recorder demonstrates to student teachers the positive aspects of their teaching as well as areas that need improvement. One aspect the videocassette can show, which perhaps only a "camera" can reveal, is that the student teacher is older than the students. Student teachers see themselves interacting with students and understand that they are not as close in age to students as they may feel they are. Hopefully, they see themselves as professionals, set apart from their students.

Videotaping is not a new experience for most student teachers. Many have been videotaped during microteaching sessions in their general methods or special methods courses on campus. No matter how often the university supervisor recommends that student teachers be videotaped, the first taping should occur after they have had time to become familiar with students, classroom procedures, and methodology. Hopefully, this will ensure initial gains in their self-confidence as teachers will not be destroyed.

For best results in using the videocassette recorder, Lang, Quick, and Johnson (1981) suggest the following:

> Predetermine what is to be filmed . . . secure mutual, advance, student and supervising teacher agreement on purpose and procedures . . . use it frequently [to avoid conditioning] . . . use it as a conferencing (analysis) tool . . . and require the student teacher to use it for self-analysis. (p. 114)

Audiocassette Recorder

The audiocassette recorder is the last observation tool described in this chapter. It has several advantages. First, it is easily accessible. Second, it affords student teachers an opportunity to listen to themselves. They can analyze their speech patterns, voice inflection and volume, and questioning techniques. Third, student teachers can listen to the tape in privacy. And fourth, student teachers begin the process of self-analysis early in their career.

A disadvantage is that the nonverbal expressions of the students and student teacher or the student teacher's mobility cannot be observed.

This chapter does not address what student teachers might observe in addition to their own teaching. It is important for student teachers to observe physical, instructional, and management characteristics of school personnel as well as extracurricular, community, and professional characteristics. Books such as Devor's (1964) *The Experience of Student Teaching*, Henry and Beasley's (1989) *Supervising Student Teachers the Professional Way*, and Lang, Quick, and Johnson's (1981) *A Partnership for the Supervision of Student Teachers* are helpful in providing suggestions for structuring such observations.

In conclusion, the purpose of observing is to monitor growth and modify instructional behavior. To do this, university supervisors utilize formal and informal communication and observation techniques; observe specific professional competencies and personal qualities; and select specific techniques of observation to provide meaningful feedback appropriate to each situation. Effective supervisors are acutely aware that different approaches to observation may be required for each student teacher.

Chapter 8 ————————————————————————————

Evaluating Student Teachers

University supervisors are engulfed by evaluation. An understanding of evaluation responsibilities, including legal parameters in evaluating student teachers, is crucial. Supervisors also explain the purposes of evaluation to cooperating teachers; help student teachers engage in self-evaluation; write final evaluations; and grade student teachers.

SUPERVISORS' RESPONSIBILITIES

To whom is the university supervisor responsible when evaluating student teachers? First, the supervisor is responsible to the student teacher. Evaluation must help student teachers achieve their potential. The outcome(s) of evaluation may affect the prospective teacher's entire professional career. Therefore, an evaluation must be objective.

Second is the responsibility to the university. As long as student teachers receive credit from the university, the supervisor *is* the instructor and responsible for assessing the student teacher's performance.

Third is the responsibility to the public. Students who have gained admittance to student teaching programs deserve a chance to succeed or fail. However, it is the supervisor's responsibility to counsel inadequate students out of teaching (Nelson & McDonald, 1958).

DUE PROCESS

Evaluation requires an understanding of and the execution of legal ramifications. Henry and Beasley (1989) state, "Case law seems to affirm the principle that professionals have the right, obligation, authority and ability to evaluate teacher candidates. The courts insist that due process must be exercised" (p. 222). They list five processes that constitute due process in evaluating the student teacher:

1. Review the evaluation instrument and its interpretation with the student teacher;
2. Observe the student teacher;
3. Critique and analyze the student teacher;
4. Evaluate the student teacher continuously; and
5. Discuss the completed final evaluation form with the student teacher. (p. 222)

Reviewing the evaluation instrument and its interpretation with student teachers can be done during the seminar before student teaching begins. A copy of the form can be given to student teachers. Awareness of the criteria upon which evaluation will be made may hopefully help them to engage in self-evaluation throughout the term.

The second due process is to observe student teachers. How often you observe may depend upon your schedule, university policy, and student teachers' competencies. However, in fairness to students, you should observe as many times as necessary to write a legitimate evaluation.

The third due process is to critique and analyze student teachers. After each observation, share your feedback. Be certain that student teachers understand your criticisms. Help them set goals for improvement so that you and the student teachers may look for growth during subsequent visits.

The fourth due process, continuous evaluation, sets the climate for professionalism. Student teachers are more likely to take their professional growth more seriously. Continuous evaluation also protects university supervisors and cooperating teachers, especially in cases where student teachers may be failing. Documentation demonstrates growth or lack of growth. Aside from the legalities, accumulated notes facilitate writing the final evaluation. Relying only on one's memory can eliminate some important aspects that could influence the final written evaluation.

The last due process is to discuss the final evaluation results with student teachers. In the final conference, share your interpretation of the student teacher's strengths and areas to improve on. Provide suggestions for professional development (e.g., a student teacher who had major discipline problems may be advised to take a workshop on "Discipline and Classroom Management" or a shy and timid student may be advised to enroll in an "Assertiveness Training" course). During the conference, allow time for the student teacher to comment on your evaluation. Some university policies provide an opportunity for the student teacher to have input as to what is included in the final evaluation. Whatever your institutional policy is, be sure to take time to discuss the "why's" of your comments.

Implementing these processes is the responsibility of both the university supervisor and cooperating teacher. Therefore, a priority of the supervisor must be to inform cooperating teachers of their responsibility to evaluate student teachers. The supervisor also interprets any additional university policy for evaluating. This interpretation may include explanations of the philosophy of evaluation and assessment processes such as self-evaluation, student evaluation of the student teacher, writing final evaluations, and grading.

PURPOSES OF EVALUATION

What might university supervisors tell students and cooperating teachers about the purposes of evaluation? They may say that it serves several purposes. One purpose has been mentioned previously—to help student teachers become the best teacher they are capable of becoming. This is not an easy task, but it can be accomplished by employing all the concepts described in this book.

Second, they may say that evaluation keeps the student teaching experience from becoming trial-and-error learning (Bennie, 1972). Continuous evaluation provides for specific goal setting. Achieving these goals results in the type of teaching student teachers are capable of at the completion of their student teaching experiences.

Third, supervisors may tell students and cooperating teachers that the purpose of evaluation is to help prospective employers understand the probable effectiveness of the student as a first-year teacher. Employing officials sometimes need to be reminded that a student who has only taught for a term cannot be compared to an experienced teacher. Some beginning teachers will not need much supervision while others may need some mentoring.

Fourth, they may say that another purpose evaluation serves is to aid university faculty in understanding what content might be included in the courses they teach. This is especially true for methods teachers and others who are involved in the formal preparation of teachers.

And finally, supervisors may tell cooperating teachers that a purpose of evaluation is to ensure that student teachers develop a rapport with their students and teach at their students' level of understanding.

SELF-EVALUATION

What might supervisors tell students and cooperating teachers about self-evaluation? They may tell them that objective self-evaluation leads to the improvement of teaching. One way to engage in this improvement is to keep a diary or log. Student teachers can evaluate their efforts in terms of short-range goals. For example, they may examine problems met by students, areas where additional help and preparation are needed, and their daily teaching activities. Or they may answer questions such as, "What was my most satisfying experience of the week?" "The least satisfying experience?" And "What are some ways I can build upon my experiences?" Answering these questions helps student teachers analyze their needs and provides continuous evaluation (Merriman & Fair, 1953). University supervisors may read these logs during their visits or have student teachers send them a copy each week. Supervisors may also say that student teachers can evaluate themselves through student input. Student teachers can discover such qualities as fairness, impartiality, friendliness, enthusiasm, sincerity, and so on. A typical questionnaire constructed by student teachers should have a limited number of scaled questions (one side of a sheet of paper is adequate) and a few questions requesting an expression of likes and dislikes about the teacher or course (Association for Student Teaching Yearbook, 1949). In interpreting the results, student teachers are advised to look at "trends," not one or two negative comments, and to remember that this is not a teacher rating but an evaluation of student reactions (Association for Student Teaching Yearbook, 1949). Furthermore, a student evaluation:

enables the teacher to learn what pupils are constantly saying about him to others. Once in on the secret, he is in a position to improve by eliminating the factors that stimulate the criticisms. (Association for Student Teaching Yearbook, 1949, p. 108)

Using student input as a tool of self-evaluation may help get a point across that the university supervisor and cooperating teacher tried but failed to communicate.

WRITING FINAL EVALUATIONS

What might university supervisors tell cooperating teachers about writing final evaluations? First, supervisors may tell them that evaluation forms may be unstructured (descriptive statements) or structured (checklist type) or a combination of the two. Whatever form you use, keep in mind that employers appreciate knowing about specific strengths and actual accomplishments of prospective teachers. Generalities are not helpful (e.g., "he did well in teaching geography"). Neither are flowery statements (e.g., "she magnificently taught superbly planned lessons every day"). They may get the job done but could also boomerang upon the writer. A neighboring district who hires the teacher candidate may not find her at all like you described her, placing your credibility at risk.

Second, supervisors may tell cooperating teachers that they should be open-minded, frank, and honest. Cooperating teachers need to keep in mind that what they write is going to be a permanent record and affects the beginning of the student teacher's professional career. The advice that Merriman and Fair gave in 1953 about writing statements for final evaluations is still true today. They stated:

> In those instances where students are not strong or have definite weaknesses, the statements in the evaluation record are a protection to the college from the employer who might otherwise ask, "Why did you not warn us?" [And], . . . straightforward statements are also a protection to the student, for in some cases employers should not expect the beginning teacher to carry heavy responsibilities until he has established confidence through his strengths . . . (p. 10)

Finally, university supervisors may tell cooperating teachers that when writing an evaluation, they should consider at least the following influences: the uniqueness of the assignment; the level(s) of teaching; the amount of freedom given in the assignment; and the student teacher's personality.

Institutional policy may require that the student teacher's permanent credential file contain separate evaluations written by both the university supervisor and the cooperating teacher, or a jointly written evaluation, or one written by the supervisor, who incorporates comments from the cooperating teacher. Whether supervisors are advising cooperating teachers or writing an evaluation jointly, they must remain open-minded and flexible because cooperating teachers may have differing standards. But in all cases, it is the supervisor's responsibility to make sure that the final written evaluations to be placed in the student's file are fair and just.

GRADING

What should university supervisors know about grading student teachers? First, supervisors should think about how they would answer the following questions: Why are grades necessary for student teaching? What factors should be considered in grading the student teacher's efforts? What weight should these factors contribute to the grade? And how should progress be graded? Is the grade an average of achievement throughout the term or is it based upon the teaching abilities demonstrated during the last one or two weeks?

Second, as stated earlier in this chapter, supervisors should know that it is their responsibility to assess the performance of the student teacher. In many instances, supervisors take into consideration the cooperating teacher's recommendations for a grade. But it is unheard of to have the cooperating teacher solely responsible for assigning the grade. Personnel other than university supervisors may be responsible for assigning grades. For example, at St. Olaf College in Northfield, Minnesota, the director of student teaching assigns the student teacher's final grade. The director considers recommendations for grades from generalists and specialists, as well as comments written on final evaluations from all supervisors and cooperating teachers. Grades are discussed with each student teacher in a final exit conference.

Third, supervisors should know that grades may reflect the student teacher's growth, potential as a teacher, and ability at the end of student teaching (Bennie, 1972). Some institutional policies require a letter grade be assigned while others employ a pass/no credit system. It is perhaps easier to grade the student teacher under the P/NC system—either the student has the teaching skills and personal qualities to be a teacher or she does not. Under the letter grade system, the supervisor's assessment is a more difficult task. What differentiates an "A" from an "$A-$" student or an "$A-$" from a "$B+$" student? Unfortunately, no matter how objective the supervisor tries to be, subjectivity sometimes reigns in making the distinction between the "A" and "B" student.

If it seems as though we are writing in generalities and providing the reader with no concrete specific advice, the reader's perception is correct. As educators we each have standards for evaluating and grading students. One method is no more right than another. It is imperative though that supervisors understand their own basis for assessment so that they are able to defend the written evaluation and grade.

In many ways it is difficult to address evaluation and observation separately because one implies the other. But for practical purposes, we differentiated between them in the last chapter. We emphasized that supervisors should create an atmosphere conducive to "observing" rather than "evaluating" since this process is usually less stressful for the student teacher and is perceived as a time to monitor growth and modify instructional behavior. This process diminishes the connotation of "finality" that the concept of evaluation has with some people. Even so, evaluation is indeed an ongoing process. We only hope that supervisors consider establishing a climate for observing rather than evaluating during each visit.

Supervisors can find additional information on assessing teacher performance in Glickman's (1990) *Supervision of Instruction: A Developmental Approach*, Henry and Beasley's (1989) *Supervising Student Teachers the Professional Way*, and Oliva's (1989) *Supervision for Today's Schools*.

Chapter 9 _____

Effective Supervisory Conferences

What is a student teacher conference? Who is involved? What occurs when one is held? These are a few of the questions that this chapter will address.

Conferences are meetings in which university supervisors, cooperating teachers, and student teachers consult with each other to share information, establish personal rapport, evaluate class performances, give and accept constructive criticism, and so on. Conferences may be formal or informal but need to be designed to ensure that everyone's perceptions are similar. The primary purpose is to provide an opportunity for evaluating past performances, to analyze what has transpired, and to help plan constructively for the future. It is a time for building trust and mutual respect. Those involved must be sensitive to each others' feelings, perceptions, personalities, and problems, and must strengthen, support, and reinforce one another.

To facilitate effective conferences, university supervisors need to analyze situations in a clinical yet positive fashion, and listen without interruption. They need to be acutely aware of a student teacher's feelings and perceptions, and they need to model the maturity and poise necessary for mediation when personalities conflict. The university supervisor must help individuals work together on a professional level in a stressful situation and do so in such a way that progress can be achieved.

Student teacher conferences present many challenges for university supervisors. Supervisors must frequently counsel student teachers who are threatened, ashamed, embarrassed, mentally and physically exhausted, stubborn, overconfident, or just plain ignorant. They must at times deal with tears, anger, guilt, and distorted views of reality. And they must always do this while always operating on "foreign turf," without a classroom of their own, without the security of a personal office, without lesson plans, and without an opportunity to prepare in advance for problems that may occur.

Most conferences can be classified under the following categories:

Initial campus conferences

Initial conferences in the host school

Conferences following classroom observation

Mid-term conferences

Final conferences

INITIAL CAMPUS CONFERENCES

The initial conference is extremely important. Prior to it, the university supervisor examines the student teacher's academic transcript, the application form, letters of recommendation, and possibly the student's autobiography. Some student files may include special requests for placement; requests for assignments in specific subject matter fields; or information concerning a health problem or physical disability that may require special placement. Thus, before meeting the student teacher, the university supervisor forms a mental profile of the student.

The initial conference provides an opportunity for the student teacher and the university supervisor to become acquainted. It is a time to explore special interests, hobbies, and any experiences student teachers have had in working with school-age children. Building upon mutual interests provides a climate in which rapport, respect, trust, and confidence in each other can grow. Each can begin to develop a perception of how the other responds. The conference forms a foundation upon which the clinical experience will evolve and mature.

It is critical that student teachers and university supervisors build a high level of trust. Student teachers who are experiencing difficulty with their assignment need to feel comfortable in contacting the university supervisor and sharing a problem. They need to feel confident that it will be treated with sincerity and confidentiality.

At the initial campus conference, it is important for university supervisors to clearly describe university policy with regard to expectations of student teachers. It is necessary that each understand the other's role. Areas of concern and need for awareness might include:

• expectations of the university for the assignment in the host school, including the number of classes to be taught;
• hours to be spent in the host school each day;
• policy concerning involvement in extracurricular activities or organizations;
• policy relating to absences or late arrivals, including who should be contacted at the host school if the student teacher is unable to arrive at school in time;
• policy relating to outside work during student teaching;
• importance of secondary student teachers not dating their students while student teaching;
• importance of belonging to a professional teacher organization;
• university policy concerning the student teacher acting as a substitute teacher or conducting class without a substitute teacher in the classroom; and,
• policy concerning coaching during student teaching, especially in a school other than one in the host school.

Students may have such questions of their own as: Where is the school? How do I get there? What's my teacher like? When do I report? To whom do I report? What do I wear? Do I eat with students or teachers? Such questions may seem trivial but are not to student teachers.

Most teacher education programs have prepared a student teacher handbook that defines university expectations for the clinical experience. While a good student teacher handbook covers most contingencies, not all student teachers interpret what is written in the same way. An explanation of these policies and expectations, in a one-to-one or group situation, reinforces the handbook statements. University supervisors need to allow time for student teachers to ask questions concerning information presented.

Many student teachers underestimate the time and energy student teaching demands and need to be reminded of all policies having an effect on their time resources. One area in particular that often needs to be mentioned and clarified is the academic load carried while student teaching. Some universities prohibit overload classes while others allow academic overload in extenuating circumstances.

Student teacher candidates often begin student teaching with information that may not be in line with university policy. Some may have made time commitments (working, coaching, etc.) that will not be possible to keep if they are to fulfill university and host school expectations. A few may try to twist the interpretations of school policy for their own benefit. If the supervisor, in the initial conference, can eliminate misconceptions, the clinical experience is more likely to be successful and enjoyable for all.

INITIAL CONFERENCES IN THE HOST SCHOOL

During the initial conference in the host school, the university supervisor, cooperating teacher, and student teacher begin the development of their professional relationship. A good place to start is an examination of the student teacher's schedule, including a discussion of the class load, the feasibility of assisting the cooperating teacher with some of his or her assigned responsibilities (playground, bus, lunchroom duty, and study hall supervision), and observations in other teachers' classrooms. Finally, host school regulations need to be clarified and a time for future meetings should be set.

For the student teacher, the initial conference provides an

opportunity to check perceptions. "Yes, I will teach three classes in social studies." "I will start with the reading classes and progress through all subjects, culminating in the last two weeks by teaching the entire day in fifth grade." "Yes, I am expected to keep staff hours, which means I will be here at 7:10 each morning and can leave after 3:45 each afternoon." "If I cannot reach school by 7:30, I will first call my cooperating teacher and then call the school secretary." It is vital that each share a common understanding of what is expected regarding duties, participation, and evaluation.

Criteria for classroom observation by university supervisors is also established during the conference. Usually there are questions such as, "Will you notify me before you make an observation?" "How long will you stay?" "If I am having a bad day, will you stay the whole period?" "How do I introduce you to my class?" "Do we meet after the lesson, the class, or after school?" Such questions need to be answered early to reduce some of the uncertainty of classroom observation procedures.

The initial conference in the host school sets the ground rules for the student teacher, the cooperating teacher, and the university supervisor. It is an excellent opportunity for creating a team concept designed to provide the best possible framework for success, not only for the student teacher but for the students in the classroom. Student teachers need confidence in those who will be guiding them throughout the clinical experience. If perception of their involvement is positive, it can relieve stress, permit experimentation with learning strategies and teaching techniques, and provide an opportunity for increased involvement.

CONFERENCES FOLLOWING
CLASSROOM OBSERVATIONS

As stated in Chapter 7, there are two basic ways to conduct classroom observations. First, supervisors can arrange to visit a specific class, indicating both time and day. Student teachers then have ample opportunity to prepare a specific lesson using a selected teaching strategy. Second, university supervisors make nonscheduled visits to the classroom, the rationale being that then a typical class situation is observed. Each strategy has merit.

University supervisors should indicate before observing a class what strategies will be used. They must always be aware that their presence can change the attitude and behavior of the students. A positive message is communicated to students in the classroom and the student teacher if university supervisors appear to be at ease, friendly, and interested in what the class is doing. A negative message is sent, however, if the supervisor reads a book, gazes out the window, applies cosmetics, looks bored, or engages in conversation with the cooperating teacher. (In lab courses, such as physical education and art, conversation *may* be appropriate during student activities.) Supervisors must present a positive involved image to everyone in the classroom to justify giving comments and constructive criticism during the post-observation conference.

Each conference following a classroom observation deals with the student teacher's performance and is unique for each situation. Usually, the ideal time for the conference is immediately following the observation when the lesson is fresh in the minds of both the university supervisor and the student teacher.

How much time should be allowed for a conference following an observation? The length of the conference is usually based on what occurred during the observation. If all went well, the conference may be short, reinforcing the positive that took place. If an audio or video tape is to be reviewed, or a formal evaluation strategy was used, the time required might exceed an hour. If a situation was observed that needs more explanation and input from the university supervisor, additional time might be needed. Occasionally, student teachers might need to regain their poise and confidence before being able to discuss what happened during the observation, and the post-observation conference might have to be postponed for an hour or two.

The conference following the observation is critical. It provides an opportunity for all to clarify any misconceptions. The setting should provide privacy. The conference should follow a format designed to build trust and maintain confidentiality. Usually it begins with the positive elements observed in the class. This may include statements such as, "Your class was very motivated today." "You did an excellent job using higher order questions." "Your use of cooperative learning strategies was excellent." "The class discussion involved nearly all of your students. Good." Many times excellent results occur when student teachers do most of the talking. Possibly they were following instructions or procedures that were new to them and something the cooperating teacher may have recommended. Maybe a film or video tape did not arrive in time and they had to improvise at the last minute. Lack of participation by the class or their inability to focus on a task could be the result of an approaching school event or activity.

University supervisors can vary the strategy by asking student teachers to relate what they perceived to be the positive aspects of the class. If there are differences, it is good strategy to explore both views. For example, student teachers might feel they had the total attention of the class and that all students were on task, but the supervisor might have observed notes being passed, students gazing out the window, and books other than the text being read.

As the conference progresses, each aspect of the observation can be explored. How does the student teacher get the undivided attention of the class before beginning the lesson? Was the forty-five-minute lecture appropriate for seventh-grade students? How can a slow reader be motivated to read aloud? Should a poor math student be asked to work a problem at the blackboard? Are students allowed to pass notes during class? Is gum chewing permitted? How much movement and noise interferes with the learning process? The supervisor must always remember that it is easy to be overcritical when documenting classroom behavior, especially when he or she is not involved directly in the teaching and classroom management process.

An observer must also remember that student teachers are novices in the process of developing skills, poise, and confidence, which the observer most likely already possesses. For each criticism, a remedy should be offered.

Each conference following a classroom observation should end on a positive note. Regardless of how the class went, the student teacher did something worthy of praise. If what was observed left something to be desired, determine together what can be salvaged and built upon for the next class. If criticism is necessary, it must be given in a constructive way. University supervisors must be aware of their behavior, tone of voice, and even body language when dispensing constructive criticism. Add a harsh tone, an unsmiling face, or an aggressive posture to criticism, and it is easy to predict the outcome of the conference, especially if a student teacher lacks self-confidence. Some student teachers are more mature and capable of accepting constructive criticism without being defensive. It helps to have a few of these student teachers so you do not always have to weigh every word.

On occasion, it is advisable to have the cooperating teacher(s) present during the post-observation conference. Many times they can provide input that directly affects the interpretation of the university supervisor. If the lesson went well, they can share in the positive evaluation. If the lesson did not meet expectations, the cooperating teacher(s) can provide input regarding why the planned strategy failed, or why the class did not participate, or why interruptions occurred. Perhaps the cooperating teachers will recommend a particular teaching strategy. Possibly, they will suggest a technique to be used in dealing with a disruptive student. If cooperating teachers have input during the conference, there is an opportunity for building understanding and support between them and the student teachers.

Following the conference, it is a good practice for university supervisors to check their perceptions with the cooperating teacher(s). Input from them is very important, as they may see the behavior of the student teacher differently because they see his or her day-to-day progress. The supervisor may ask questions such as, "I noticed her making the same error in grammar twice today. Is this a pattern?" "He has excellent lesson plans, complete with reasonable goals. Today, however, he read from notes most of the period. Is his academic background weak or was he just nervous?" "Today she had a problem with three girls in the back of the class. Has this happened before?" "I had trouble hearing him several times during his class discussion. Does he usually speak that quietly?" As a team, with similar perceptions of the student teacher's ability, the cooperating teacher and university supervisor can offer constructive criticism in an acceptable manner. By supporting the other's efforts, emerging patterns can be detected. The shared observation can then be communicated to the student teacher with greater emphasis.

It is best for the post-observation conference to be held soon after the observation in a place that affords privacy. This way student teachers do not have to wonder for the next few hours what the university supervisor thought of their teaching. Hopefully, the cooperating teacher(s) will also be present. And if the same lesson is to be taught to another class, the conference could indicate strategies that might strengthen the next presentation.

MIDTERM CONFERENCES

Students deserve to know where they stand in regard to success or lack of success during the clinical experience. The midterm conference offers an opportunity to review progress to date. The midterm conference and evaluation identify areas of strength as well as those areas that need more concentration and effort. Student teachers have the right to expect input on how their performance may be improved in order to receive the best possible final evaluation. This conference also provides an opportunity for perception checks to ensure that each individual involved in the student teaching experience is communicating effectively.

Goals and objectives for personal and professional growth can be examined. Questions such as, "Do you feel more comfortable in a leadership role now?" "Are you seeing the differences between third and sixth grade?" "You seem to be more poised and confident in the classroom. Do you feel that way?" may be used to initiate their participation.

One of the most important factors of the midterm conference is to realize that student teachers are under stress. They are teaching in a classroom that is not theirs. They have limited legal standing as teachers. They are trying to please their cooperating teachers and university supervisors. Students in their classrooms may or may not choose to cooperate during observations. University supervisors need to remember to offer encouragement and positive reinforcement that tells student teachers they are worthy, contributing individuals.

The midterm evaluation is a statement of achievement. It may be a written document, a formal evaluation form with checklists, or a continuum indicating progress in comparison to what is desired, a combination of both, or an oral review. It is documentation of the student teacher's achievements and progress (or lack of them). It is an opportunity for university supervisors and cooperating teachers to recommend ways in which the student teacher might improve during the remainder of the student teaching experience. (It might be noted that some excellent university supervisors provide an evaluation update each visit and choose not to use a formal midterm evaluation.)

THE FINAL CONFERENCE

The final conference is usually held between the student teacher and the university supervisor. It may take place in the host school or at the university. On occasion, it might include the cooperating teachers. Typically, it includes a review of the final evaluation written by cooperating teachers and university supervisors. The final evaluation is a document that summarizes the student teaching experience. There may be a letter grade attached to it or it may be submitted in lieu of a final grade. It states what was accomplished, the basis for the evaluation, their successes as a student teacher in the classroom, and any other pertinent information such as involvement in extracurricular activities, tutoring, assisting in sponsoring student activities, leadership qualities, rapport with students and staff, organizational competence, planning, and ability to evaluate student progress.

During the final conference, university supervisors should provide an opportunity for student teachers to examine their final evaluation. If questions arise, supervisors should be able to support what is written. In addition, during the final conference, student teachers should have an opportunity to share information about their host schools, cooperating teachers, those who should be considered as future cooperating teachers, and especially what university supervisors could do to enhance the clinical experience for the next group of student teachers.

One of the most important aspects of the final conference is for university supervisors to help student teachers think about their future. Do they really like working with children enough to make teaching a profession? Which grade level do they prefer? Is the grade level more important than where or what they teach? What skills might they improve upon to be more successful in the classroom? Have they planned to seek a job in the immediate area? Have they considered geographic areas where demand exceeds supply? In essence, now that student teachers have finished their professional training, the university supervisor helps them consider career options.

Student teaching conferences are important. At all times, university supervisors must keep in mind that student teaching deals with personalities in a stressful situation. They must be flexible in their approach, sensitive to the needs of others, and willing to make decisions necessary to facilitate a positive, successful experience for each student teacher. If ever in doubt as how to deal with a stressful situation, one where poise and confidence have been challenged, university supervisors should put themselves in the place of the student teacher and ask, "How would I like my university supervisor to treat this situation?"

The University Supervisor as Seminar Teacher

Seminars during student teaching are generally held after school hours and are conducted by the university supervisor. Most universities also provide a seminar prior to sending student teachers to school assignments.

The quality of seminars is an important variable in determining the quality of student teaching. For some student teachers, seminars are the frosting on the cake—an activity making their experience even more special. For others, they are a place where questions can be answered, a time for airing frustrations, a reference point for marking progress, a chance to put growth into perspective, and an opportunity to discover their uniqueness. Some dread and use every excuse possible to avoid them.

During seminars, we have seen wallflowers blossom, the boisterous become mellow, the closed-minded become tolerant, and the self-centered become "other" directed. Part of these changes resulted from student teaching itself but some occurred because of the seminar. When student teachers open themselves and share concerns with those who accept, listen, and do not judge, miraculous things occur.

Seminars can be a precious time, but like all precious moments they can be easily shattered. One or two students who cannot think of much besides beer and parties or one or two who dominate or are incredibly immature can up end the best-laid plans.

The first step toward conducting a successful seminar, then, is to help the group members understand the potential of the seminar and why it could be of personal and professional importance to them. The second step is to keep shortsighted individuals in need of instant gratification from destroying an experience that has potential for growth.

If we take four hours of a student's time (one hour driving each way included), what we do, and offer, and the climate we create should be good and something they cannot easily obtain elsewhere. How you conduct a seminar, the environment you encourage, the questions you ask, the tone of your own responses, the input you allow—all of this and more—will depend upon your disposition, knowledge, and perceptions.

The university supervisor who believes that student teaching is a student's most important term in college, that a student teacher is as receptive to change and is as pliable as a sixth grader going into junior high or as a senior going away to college, and that openness, honesty, and respect must be modeled to be taught, would conduct his or her seminars quite differently than a university supervisor who believes, with equal vigor, the opposite—that is, that student teaching is only another term; a seminar is just an evening class; and values and attitudes change very little after age five. We encourage you to use the seminar to accomplish goals not accomplishable elsewhere—as a time to fill in the gaps and provide essential knowledge not previously presented or comprehended.

With the possible exception of the first seminar (it will be discussed later in this chapter), the one held before students go to their schools, seminars should be used for small-group work and discussions. It is not a time for lectures. Such information can be written and distributed before or after class. Nor is it a time to listen to guest speakers, especially if such persons can be accessed during school hours. Seminars should be used to address immediate concerns of student teachers and used as a forum for student teachers to think aloud and talk intelligently and precisely. It is important that we use this time wisely and know what we are doing and why we are doing it.

A typical seminar might be conducted as follows: The first portion would be used for the airing and sharing of student questions, personal concerns, problems, successes, insights, growth, and opinions. Some examples are:

"I (a male) walked into the girls' bathroom by mistake."

"A student told me she finally understood. I am on a cloud."

"When should I call a student's parents?"

"How many warnings do I give before sending a student to the principal?"

"A third grade student asked, 'Will you start dating my mom because the guys she has been dating are such 'nerds.' "

"When do you know your students well enough to know what works?"

"I just asked Midge and Bill not to talk and looked them right in the eye and it worked!"

"Last term student teachers told us to 'always have extra materials prepared for class.' At our first seminar you told us to 'always prepare more than you think you'll need for the hour—be overprepared.' In spite of this sound advice, I still ran out of material."

"Two notes have been left on my desk, both propositioning me."

"What do the rest of you do about the heavy, and I mean *heavy*, necking in the halls?"

The second portion would focus on a problem suggested by student teachers earlier in the term, a question several students bring up that evening, or a recent news story or an item you wish to discuss, perhaps something that you have observed over and over while visiting schools. The topic, as long as it is relevant, is not nearly as important as the process used to discuss it. Some examples of topics are:

Is teaching what you expected?

How do you show respect and get respect from your students?

What things have challenged your ingenuity this week?

My cooperating teacher hates teaching and does not try to hide it.

What is reasonable, what is too much, and what is too little?

The last portion of the seminar would be used to provide a brief summary of what transpired during the past two hours and to develop assignments for the next seminar. Some examples are:

Ask your principal if a social life can be completely separated from a professional life.

Ask your cooperating teacher how to handle the apathetic child who does not care about grades or whether you involve parents. Also ask him or her about the relationship between humor and discipline problems.

Find out how three different teachers in your building handle the student who talks back.

Next week bring your own thoughts about whether a teacher should be consistent and predictable. Also bring a list of the rituals and routines you see in teaching.

Before the next seminar, sprint write for two minutes about how you are helping your students satisfy their basic need to be needed.

Think about these two items: "Is punishing in public a waste of time?" and "Should praise be done in private?" Come prepared to respond.

Next week bring your notes regarding what you learned from listening to your audio tape and viewing the video tape of your teaching and we will discuss them.

During seminars everyone is given a chance to share. Those with a tendency to take over are strongly encouraged, verbally and by gestures, to speak less. And, if necessary, the more reluctant students are called upon.

At some point during the seminar, students are randomly grouped. Since they generally sit beside those with whom they car pool and have already talked to them before getting to the seminar and will talk to them while going home, we usually number students off. Often, however, we group those born during the same month, those with the same majors, or those teaching at the same grade levels.

After students have been in their groups of no more than five persons for a maximum of fifteen minutes, they are asked to share one or two of the insights they gained during their discussion. Early in the period, we also ask them how their group is functioning. "Did someone do all of the talking? If so, tell them to listen more. Remind them that there are four other people in the group, all of whom need to share." "Did any of you try to draw out the quiet ones in your group?" "Did you stick to the assignment at hand?" Groups work well if we do our best to ensure that all members get an equal opportunity to share.

What should they talk about in these groups? Sometimes it is beneficial to discuss things foremost on their minds. Some tend to do this anyway, but generally a direction and a focus need to be given (i.e., "What did you learn about yourself this week?" "Are you more patient than you previously believed?" "As a teacher what did you learn this week?" "Why do many teachers hate interruptions, such as students coming in late, students needing to leave for band lessons, announcements made over the intercom, and so on?").

During seminars the university supervisor's comments are kept brief. Notes are taken so if a discussion strays, students can be reminded of the issue being addressed. The university supervisor bites a pencil to keep from talking, directs verbal traffic with hand gestures, cups a hand to the ear to encourage the timid to speak more loudly, occasionally calls on people, and sometimes tells one or two to let others talk. It is amazing how great discussions become when an atmosphere of trust is created, when the supervisor shuts up and keeps the few from dominating, and when the supervisor does not offer any views until the end of the discussion.

During discussions, student teachers are reminded that the university supervisor is only one member of the group, and eye contact should be maintained, about equally, with everyone. To facilitate more input from all and to help everyone realize that the most shy and soft-spoken often have brilliant insights to offer, a Japanese Discussion is used. A Japanese Discussion, a term used by Alice Miel at Teachers College, is simply a method that allows all students to talk before anyone who has already talked gets a chance to speak again. This method stifles spontaneity, but if notes are taken, this spontaneity as well as the most important reactions can be rekindled and discussed after all have had their say.

Before closing, a few words about the first seminar, which is held on campus before student teaching begins. This first seminar is the most important one you will have all term. It is the one where you are "sized up," and where it is decided if you can be trusted to be a decent, fair, and reliable individual.

At the end of the seminar, encourage your students to critique, evaluate, and assign you a final grade. Remember, however, that they are experts in the art of seeing through insincerity, and your nonverbal behavior is communicated so precisely and completely that what you say is secondary to how you say it. If what you say and how you say it are inconsistent you will be judged accordingly as a phony!

We are being somewhat flippant about having student teachers evaluate you, but in a sense, they do this without being given permission. Teaching is a personal, intimate, risk-taking occupation in which we expose ourselves completely. We hope that university supervisors always observe student teachers with these givens in mind!

During the first seminar we try to accomplish the following ten things:

1. Before the seminar begins but after making sure that students are in the right course, we have them sprint write for two minutes on each of the following: "While you were sitting here waiting for class to start, what thoughts were running through your mind?" "Were your thoughts the same as those your students will have when you teach that first day? Are they different? How?" "Are you going to introduce yourself to your class tomorrow? If so what exactly will you say? "How do you plan to keep from jumping to premature conclusions?"

2. We learn our students' names and have them learn each others' names. This is not difficult if the desire to do so is present. However, we *have* to want to do it, and we *have* to hear the name correctly and clearly. We do not forget names, we just do not learn them in the first place. Some will need to write the name down and say it aloud and repeat it several times. Even people who are the very best at remembering names do these things. We have all learned thousands of bits of information to get where we are, so the problem is not one of intelligence. It is a matter of how important we believe others to be. The correlation between student teachers with disci-

pline problems and student teachers who do not know their students' names is astounding. Student teachers with discipline problems not only do not know their students' names but frequently cannot remember who was sitting where or who was wearing what. They are so self-absorbed, self-directed, and concerned about how they are doing that their caring for students, if indeed it exists, is not communicated. We tell them to at least care enough about their peers to learn their names.

3. We discuss expectations—theirs, ours, and their cooperating teachers'. Nothing gets us into more trouble than expecting something and not having that expectation met. People have gone into a depression for weeks over such matters. We ask them what they want, need, and expect from us. We ask them what their cooperating teacher should have a right to expect from them, what makes cooperating teachers pleased about student teachers, and what makes them extremely upset. And we tell them what we expect— punctuality; to call the school and make sure that their cooperating teachers get the message if they have to be absent; to dress appropriately; to attend seminars; to fill out the forms, address cards, and sign-up sheets; and to report concerns, complaints, and suggestions from cooperating teachers so that we, as university supervisors, might improve. We require them to go out into the schools as learners, to give student teaching their very best effort, and to call us if they really have problems so we can have time to think about a professional response before arriving at their school.

4. We discuss attitudes. We tell them that their student teaching experience depends upon their attitudes, and we encourage them to state the attitudes they will take into student teaching.

5. We answer any of their questions and concerns (i.e., "Who do I report to when I get to my school tomorrow morning?" "How often will you visit?" "Will you want to see my lesson plans?").

6. We discuss professionalism, personality, and outstanding teaching. We ask what they would see an outstanding teacher do if they were observing them, how they would describe a teacher with an excellent personality, and what professional behavior they most admire.

7. We ask them to list three things they would like us to look for when we observe them teach that first time or the three things they would most like to learn about themselves this term.

8. We ask them what specific things they might observe during the first week of their student teaching (i.e., "What does the teacher

do with those who finish a test early?" "How, specifically, does the teacher use praise?" "How many seconds does the teacher wait after asking a question before calling upon a student?" "What class routines and expectations does the teacher seem to have?")

9. We ask them to discuss their hopes and aspirations and to be honest when answering, "I am becoming a teacher because . . ."

10. We discuss how they will be evaluated, have them say a few words about themselves, and ask them to list what they believe to be the five most common student teaching mistakes.

We try to accomplish four goals during the first seminar:

1. We *answer* all of their questions so they can leave with as much self-confidence and sense of control as possible.

2. We *present* ourselves as caring, compassionate, and understanding persons who listen and are fair.

3. We also *leave* them with the understanding that we are in charge, can make decisions, and have high expectations.

4. We *set the tone* that seminars are for thinking and speaking and the best of both are demanded. We believe that high standards *do not* stifle student teacher participation.

Thirteen additional topics for seminars are:

- Resume writing
- Role playing the job interview
- Developing a list of questions for the job interview
- Questioning skills—asking higher order questions
- Parent-teacher conferences
- Working with and getting along with teachers other than your co-operating teacher
- Lesson and unit planning
- Questions to ask your cooperating teacher before you leave—how to order films, how textbooks are selected, expectations during the first week of workshops and teaching, procedures for taking field trips, and so on.
- Licensure/certification
- Grading methods

- Tests—before, after, during, grading, preparing
- The art of substituting—"Alive at Five"
- Specialists in the school—curriculum directors, nurses, special education teachers, speech pathologists, counselors, and so on.

Good luck!

Chapter 11

Working with First-time Cooperating Teachers

We forget what it is like to be fifteen. Yet when we pause for a moment, we can conjure up those memories. The same is true for our student teaching experience. Many times each term, university supervisors need to remind themselves and cooperating teachers what it is like to be a student teacher. Student teachers have not changed. They still want to do a good job, do not want to fail, and are concerned about the impressions they are making. They continue to want to develop habits and attitudes that lead to growth.

Like us, when we student taught, they face sensory overload. They wonder if they will make a fool of themselves, if students will understand what they are presenting, if they will need to make a 180-degree turn because of students' expectations, and if they will be looked upon as a "real" teacher. There are so many things for them to think about. "How will my students react to me?" "Will I have control?" "Will students respect me?"

All at the same time, they feel excitement, discomfort, fear, uncertainty, and eagerness. They are between the roles of being a teacher and a student teacher, and they believe that their cooperating teacher will be standing there double checking, ready to override them. They know that the cooperating teacher's class is not really theirs and wonder if they will be given a fair chance at discovering their own teaching style. They try to please everyone, while feeling like a guest in someone else's home. They know that they are on probation and must watch their every step and believe this pressure will never end.

When first-time cooperating teachers ask your advice, tell them that the attitudes their student teachers take into the world of teaching are determined by how they, as a cooperating teacher, relate to and treat those student teachers.

Student teachers need respect. They need to be introduced as a teacher, and they appreciate having cooperating teachers answer their questions. They respect patience, sensitivity, and acknowledgment that they have a life outside of school.

When we ask student teachers what cooperating teachers should know about college seniors and graduate students who are student teaching, again and again they tell us these ten things: 1. We expect and need criticism that will make us better teachers but we also need lots of support right away; 2. We need to know that someone is there if we have a problem; 3. We need to be allowed to experiment; 4. We need cooperating teachers who, at some point, acknowledge that this is hard for us and know this is a whole new area for us; 5. We need help finding resources; 6. We need cooperating teachers who will make sure we are ready before they make us teach; 7. We do not know everything, are still learning, and lack experience, so we need guidance; 8. We like input. Any input and advice is great; 9. We need cooperating teachers who do not expect too much from us initially; and 10. We try our best to do our best.

Trying to meet the needs of those who vacillate between dependence and independence, and between confidence and insecurity, is not a job for a "know-it-all." Student teachers are both fragile and pliable. They need to be directed with great care and sensitivity. But if handled correctly, they bloom like the most beautiful flower ever created.

When asked, "What is the one thing your cooperating teacher did that helped you the most?" student teachers' answers over the years have allowed us to create this list of twenty items: 1. They did not interfere with what I was trying to do; 2. They took me in when I needed a place to student teach; 3. They called me by my last name in front of students; 4. They let me try to figure it out myself before they stepped in; 5. They let me have input and let me know where I stood at all times; 6. They listened; 7. They were honest; 8. They guided me instead of telling me what to do; 9. They were confident in me and were positive; 10. If they thought I was doing something badly, they told me so I could stop doing it; 11. They were always there if I had a problem; 12. They gave no orders—only suggestions; 13. They were patient and talked to me in depth about certain students or techniques; 14. They let me know what I could not do so I had some ideas about my boundaries; 15. They informed me of all the school policies and showed me where everything was in the building; 16. They gave me the option of having them in the room when I started teaching or having them leave; 17. They devoted themselves to helping me learn and survive; 18. They made their materials available but did not force them upon me; 19. They gave me a desk, a place to study, a place to call my own; and 20. They supported my efforts and were concerned about how my day went—they were an excellent model and went the extra mile.

When working with first-time cooperating teachers, tell them three things: 1. Our joint goal is to help your student teacher become the best teacher he or she is capable of becoming; 2. We want your student teacher, if possible, to have a good and realistic teaching experience; and 3. We want your student teacher to leave with as much idealism in tact as possible (they will lose this quickly enough as is). Tell the new cooperating teacher that student teachers will never be any better than they think they are and that how good they think they are depends on what the cooperating teacher and you tell them. Rarely can student teachers override cooperating teachers *and* university supervisors and honestly say, "They do not know what they are talking about. I am doing just great."

Also, tell new cooperating teachers that how they handle things is up to them, that they should trust their instincts. As long as they want their student teachers to have good and realistic experiences and encourage them to be the best student teachers they are capable of becoming, they should trust their built-in guidance system. Something as complicated as being a cooperating teacher cannot be cookbooked.

When new cooperating teachers ask questions, we answer them. The following are the most frequently asked questions and the answers we most often give:

1. How often should I observe?

As often as you feel you should. You have a built-in guidance system that keeps you on target. Trust it. Also, ask your student teachers what they think. As long as you want them to become the best teachers they are capable of becoming and as long as you realize they will interact with thousands of students during their lifetime, these responsibilities will be your excellent guides.

2. What forms must I fill out?

Only the final evaluation. We want you to work with us again, so we try to be realistic about paperwork. We are fully aware you have too much paperwork already. If your student teacher wants to complete a midterm evaluation form on him or herself and then asks you to go over it with him or her, fine.

3. Do you expect them to be here from eight to four each day?

We expect whatever you decide. But, yes, the times that regular teachers are required to be at school seem reasonable. Student teaching is a full-time job and, like teaching, involves much more than just what goes on in the classroom. Before and after school, student teachers need to be available for students, for meetings, and for other school-related functions such as parent-teacher conferences. If you have a problem, please let us know as soon as possible.

4. How often will you be coming?

This term, because I have twelve student teachers in three buildings less than twenty miles from campus and have no other teaching responsibilities, I will see them once a week. (O.K., let us dream a little, please.)

5. How, specifically, are you going to operate this term?

Every university supervisor does things a bit differently. I like to get around at least twice during the first two weeks. This way problems are kept to a minimum.

During the third and fourth week, I briefly like to observe each student teacher and write down four or more things each is doing well and one or two things each needs to think about or work upon. I do not stay long, usually only fifteen minutes. If I stay longer, early in the term, I see too much and write down too many negatives. I guess I get picky. Student teachers can only work on two or three major things at a time anyway, so I stay until I see one or two things that, if improved, would have the best chance for having a long-range impact. I write down four or five things the student teacher is doing well because genuine praise seems to work best for me. If you have any suggestions that might help me be more effective, please let me know.

After a sense of trust is established, I play supervision by ear. Some student teachers need to be seen twice a week for two hours. They need a pre- and post-conference each visit, and their cooperating teachers and principals also appreciate a conference. Other student teachers, because of their talent, the talent of their cooperating teachers, the morale of the building staff, and their ability to accept and act upon suggestions, do not need to be seen as frequently or for as long.

I try always to keep in mind, however, that cooperating teachers and student teachers need to see me, need input from the outside, need someone who will notice that they exist, and need someone who will listen. I am disappointed in myself and do not feel good about the job I am doing if I do not observe each student at least five times during a ten-week period.

6. Should I stay in the room when they teach?

That is up to you and them. If you are not able to be there, will they be able to handle the class? Should the fifth week come and you still always feel needed in the classroom, there may be a problem (unless, of course, your principal has told you to be in the room at all times). If there is a problem, we will have a conference.

7. What do you expect from me?

No one can expect more from a person than they can reasonably give. We both want the same thing: a teacher who can stand up and count for something; one who can ignore what is irrelevant and focus upon matters that demand attention; one who is proud of oneself; and one with enough character to take the initiative to carry out good intentions. Student teachers develop professionalism by having us believe in them and by having us treat them as professionals.

8. How many classes should they teach and how soon?

They should teach three or four classes with at least two preps and should begin teaching as soon as you feel they are ready. The sooner the better. They have been waiting four years for this experience and sometimes, if they sit around too long, they become bored and lose their enthusiasm. (Occasionally, however, you might encounter the opposite extreme and have to push a student teacher off the perch.) Having them teach a full load during the last week, if that can be arranged, would protect them from the criticism: "You really don't know what teaching is all about because you taught only three hours each day."

9. Will you tell me when you are coming?

I often do not know myself. Sometimes I get a call from a student teacher who is having a problem, and I have to change my schedule. If I know, however, I will tell you. It is not something I try to keep secret. I will do my best to come once a week.

10. I never observe my student teacher, but I sit in the vacant room next door and listen. Should I sit in?

Ask your student teacher. He or she may think you never observe and do not care. But, yes, I would suggest you actually sit in the classroom, at least on occasion. One cooperating teacher told his class, "Look, you yahoos. I'll be in the adjacent storeroom all the time listening and observing and checking up on you so you better not goof around." Well, not even one day passed before students started getting restroom passes to check on him. When he was not there, which was most of the time, they signaled the class with a shake of the head, and "all heck" broke loose.

11. Should we let student teachers use lesson plans?

This is up to you. Your first responsibility is to your students. Can your student teachers do without your plans or are they floundering? Next year, when they teach without you, will they be able to plan on their own? That is the main question. Let me talk to them about this matter. We do not want them to be your clone, but we do not want them to have to constantly re-invent the wheel either.

12. Do you do anything in the way of planning before they get here?

Yes. But planning is left up to you. We want them to be able to plan lessons, plan for the substitute, and turn in satisfactory lesson plans for the following week. What you plan as a teacher is quite different from what a student teacher needs to plan. If you have any questions, please let them know, and I will work with them individually on planning. We want them to know that there are many kinds of plans, that no one can teach without plans, and that the less experience a teacher has, the more he or she has to plan in writing.

13. How detailed do you want their lesson plans to be?

Their plans need to be *much* more detailed than the average, experienced cooperating teacher's plans. Just like yours were probably twenty times more detailed when you student taught than they are today.

14. Is it O.K. to have them visit other classes, the counselor, the nurse, the superintendent, and so on?

Yes! Thank you for making the time for them to do so. Observing every teacher in the district is clearly carrying things to the extreme, but what you have planned leaves sufficient time for teaching. Having them attend teacher workshops and faculty meetings would also be valuable. Thank you for caring enough to help them have the best experience possible.

15. What is my role?

Your role is to prepare your student teacher for teaching as if they were going to have your son, daughter, or grandchild as their student; to reinforce behaviors that lead to improved student learning; to encourage them to develop a teaching style that works for them; to make them responsible for their own learning; and to be the best model you can be.

16. How should I introduce them to the class?

I would introduce them as Mr., Mrs., or Ms. _____and then I would say what I felt like saying. But, for gosh sakes, *do* introduce them and *do* use Mr., Mrs., or Ms. Believe it or not, we have had student teachers sit for two weeks and then have to introduce themselves. We have also had some cooperating teachers require their student teachers to call them Mr., Mrs., or Ms. in front of the class but, at the same time, to call their student teacher by their first name in front of the class.

17. What should I do when they present incorrect information?

This is a real problem. You cannot make them feel like a jerk in front of the class, but you cannot have some parent calling you all the time either. It depends upon the class and the student teacher. To be safe, talk to your student teacher after class and make sure that he or she presents the corrected information the next day. Treat him or her like you would like the principal to treat you if you made a mistake.

18. How often should I give feedback, and should I give negative feedback?

If asking your student teacher how they would like to receive feedback does not work, experiment. And, yes, there will be times when you need to give negative feedback. Tact is an art. Give criticism as you would like a friend to tell you something that you need to be told.

We do not do student teachers any favor by neglecting to tell them what they need to hear.

19. If I get a bad student teacher, will you remove him or her?

Yes. But I must tell you that student teachers sometimes want to be moved, and I tell them to wait at least two weeks before asking me to place them elsewhere. I would hope that you would also wait for two weeks. If, however, your student teacher's behavior is so bizarre that it is over the line of acceptability—if that is the case, then we will remove him or her immediately.

20. What constitutes a crisis?

If you could get fired for doing it, it is a crisis. Call me immediately, and I will be at your school by 7:30 the next morning.

21. How many extracurricular activities should I get the student teacher involved in?

Just use your judgment. We want their experience to be realistic.

22. Can we team teach?

Yes. But remember: they may get a job in a neighboring district and you do not want those teachers questioning why you did not teach them the most basic management skills. The biggest danger of team teaching is that you will do all the leading and they will do all the following, and they will not be given an opportunity to think on their feet.

23. What can we demand in terms of manners and dress?

Whatever your school requires, I will back you one hundred percent. Remember that some student teachers do not have enough money for even a dinner out or a movie. This does not mean, however, that you ever have to accept an ill-groomed student teacher.

24. Who writes their final evaluation?

Not all universities do things the same way. Some, for example, require that both the cooperating teacher and supervisor's evaluations be placed in the student's permanent credential file. Others require that only the university supervisor's evaluation be placed in the student's file, just like a letter grade. If the student desires, the cooperating teacher's evaluation may also be placed in the file. In any event, the supervisor must rely heavily upon what the cooperating teacher says because he or she is with the student teacher everyday.

25. How will I know if I am oversupervising and being paternalistic?

That question shows a lot of insight. If only we could see ourselves as others see us, we would all make a few changes. If your student teacher is unable to help you see yourself as others see you, ask others for input, leave your student teacher alone for extended periods, experiment. Some cooperating teachers *do* have trouble letting go and *do not* want their student teacher to go through the pain of making a mistake. But the question becomes what will happen to your student teacher next year when you are not around?

A few final words. Over the years, we have seen some very good student teachers nearly destroyed by inadequate supervision, and we have seen some marginal students develop into outstanding teachers because of sound supervision. When working with a first-time cooperating teacher, it is important to remember that he or she is the most important link in the student-teaching chain.

How other staff and administrators react to student teachers, how K–12 students react, how academically prepared student teachers are, and how student teachers manage their attitudes—all of these things are important to success; but the key is, was, and always will be the cooperating teacher. Cooperating teachers are the most important people in student teachers' professional lives. They determine the attitudes student teachers carry into retirement. As university supervisors, we must do our best to support these cooperating teachers efforts, encourage their patience and understanding, and listen to their successes and disappointments.

It is easy to respect, encourage, and support most cooperating teachers. They are bright, articulate, dedicated, and professional in every way. But a few—those who do not hesitate to let you know that they are more intelligent and know more about supervision than you do, those who demand that you supervise the way your predecessor did, those who avoid you, those who accuse you of spending too little time with their student teacher, and those who treat you with contempt—can hurt and anger you.

Your best reaction to this hurt and anger is to examine the way you are doing your job. Could this outspoken cooperating teacher teach you something about supervision? Could you be doing something or not doing something that causes a cooperating teacher to avoid you? Could your cooperating teachers' philosophy of supervision have merit? Learn as much as possible from the anxiety created by this anger and hurt. Anxiety is your system letting you know that a time to learn has arrived. Anxiety is your system shouting at you, "Listen to me. This is a time to grow. Take advantage of it!"

Fortunately, cooperating teachers who accuse you unjustly, question your professionalism, and turn their student teacher against you are rare. You may only work with one or two a year.

Your best defense against them is to be a positive, kind, and understanding listener. Some, odd as it may seem, are good cooperating teachers. They just do not work well with someone from the outside or with someone who is of nearly equal status.

One last bit of advice. All of us have a conception of an effective teacher that guides our teaching behavior. Try not to let this get in your way. Try also to encourage first-time cooperating teachers to not let their conception of an effective teacher get in their way. Not everyone can or *should* teach the way we or they do. Good teaching is always good teaching but never do two teachers teach the exact same way.

Chapter 12 _____

Discipline and the University Supervisor: Developing Appropriate Attitudes

Discipline is the number-one concern of nearly every student teacher. Cooperating teachers also realize its importance. Both know that success hinges upon classroom control. What should university supervisors know about this topic, and what might they teach student teachers about discipline?

Answers to these questions constitute the content of this chapter. Discipline is as complicated as teaching itself. Controlling a class does not depend upon a quick fix like proximity control, with-it-ness, a time-out room, or writing a name upon the board. Rather, success depends upon the student teacher's *attitude.*

All classrooms, students, schools, and teachers are unique; arrange these in as many combinations as possible, and millions of appropriate and inappropriate ways to handle discipline emerge. No list of "dos and don'ts," no matter how long, or bag of tricks, no matter how full, will provide an answer to every problem in every situation. That is why discipline is so complicated and why it remains the biggest student teacher concern. That is also why many universities do not offer an undergraduate course in it. They believe that effective discipline can only be learned in the classroom and that an on-campus class in discipline would only offer false security.

It would be appropriate for student teachers, at some point, to learn more about Alfred S. Alschuler's (1980) *Social Literacy Training*; Don Dinkmeyer's and Gary D. McKay's (1980) *Systematic Training for Effective Teaching*; James Dobson's (1970) *Dare to Discipline*; Rudolf Dreikurs and P. Cassell's (1972) *Discipline Without Tears*; William Glasser's (1965) *Reality Therapy*; Thomas Gordon's (1974) *Teacher Effectiveness Training*; and Richard M. Mallory's (1980) *The Least Approach to Discipline*. It would also be very helpful for them to read some of the material written by C. M. Charles (1989) *Building Classroom Discipline, 3rd Edition*, Daniel L. Duke's and A. M. Meckel's (1984) *Teacher's Guide to Classroom Management*, Ken Ernst's (1972) *Games Students Play (And What To Do About Them)*, Alvyn M. Freed's (1976) *T. A. For Teens (And Other Important People)*, Vernon F. Jones's (1980) *Adolescents with Behavior Problems; Strategies for Teaching, Counselling, and Parent Involvement*, National School Safety Center's (1986) *School Discipline Notebook*, Southwest Texas State University's (1987) *Classroom Management and Discipline Program Manual: A Modular Text*, and Randall S. Sprick's (1985) *Discipline in the Secondary School, A Problem-by-problem Survival Guide*. These sources, and many not mentioned, offer models that provide sound, long-term advice.

Student teachers are concerned about surviving that day and the next. They are in the initial stages of forming attitudes about discipline. They wonder about such things as: Should I let a child go to the restroom, or must he or she vomit or wet on the floor for me to learn about being overly strict? When a student says "no" when asked to walk to the front of the room to give a formal speech, must I see his involuntary erection or blood on the front of her skirt before I realize there are "power struggles" I *should* lose? Did their last-year teacher actually allow them to put books away three minutes early? How can I break up a fight in the hallway? What if I tell students to go to the office, and they tell me to "go straight to hell"? Is it a good idea to not smile until Christmas? How do I walk the line between being friendly and being respected? These are the questions that student teachers ask. How they answer them now and how they resolve them in the future depends upon the attitudes they acquire during student teaching.

Student teachers have no frame of reference, no way to already know what is real and what is false. They have not been through enough cycles to sense when they are being manipulated and when they are hearing it straight. It will take time and many mistakes for them to acquire an accurate perspective. We need to help them discover what is normal. We need to keep them from becoming too cynical, and we need to give them support. When surrounded by an atmosphere of understanding and trust, student teachers learn to blow the wheat from the chaff, sort the trivial from the important, and differentiate between malicious and thoughtless acts. It takes time to gain this sense of proportion. And it takes hands-on experience in the actual classroom.

In spite of our belief that attitude is the most important variable regarding discipline, we do feel that university supervisors can teach student teachers specific things about discipline and that university supervisors can also help cooperating teachers in this area.

Our first concern is the base on which attitudes about discipline are built. This base consists of the two things that student teachers and teachers should understand and believe about discipline: first, they need to understand and believe that teachers are important—as important as anyone in any profession. Second, they need to understand and believe that discipline is the most important subject they teach.

Teachers are expected to preserve the common culture, instill common values, assimilate the immigrants, integrate the races, and serve as a substitute for the family. All of these expectations are coming from a pluralistic democratic society whose members are becoming more ethnically and linguistically diverse, more splintered, and poorer. The top 20 percent in wealth earned nine times more than the poorest 20 percent in 1986, up from seven times in 1979 (U.S. Bureau of Labor Statistics, 1988). By the year 2000, one in three public-school children will be nonwhite (Gursky, 1989), and 40 percent will come from broken homes (Wolk, 1989).

One day everyone will live, work, or recreate beside those we teach. What people value, fear, and expect from others, even the life they anticipate, will, in a large part, be learned in school.

Teachers have access to every future judge, newscaster, senator, film producer, and editor. Teachers interact with every soon-to-be influential person in our country. Teachers can turn our nation around! They can teach respect for rules, curb condescending attitudes, and arrest the trend of allowing small groups of the "big and brutal" to control the "small and weak."

Our ferociously crime-ridden society can be changed. Teachers can redirect many students' lives. Parks and interstate rest areas can be reclaimed. Grandparents can again take their grandchildren to city parks and baseball games without exposing them to profane and abusive language. Harassment on buses and subways can also be reduced. Even wilding and gangbanging can be curtailed. Teaching is an important profession!

Society expects a lot from teachers, but society also supports teachers. People in general—not just prison guards, mall security personnel, and police officers—are getting sick of spoiled, out-of-control juveniles and young adults saying and doing what they want, when they want. Even those who seem to be indifferent are getting tired of those who do not respect anyone or anything, including themselves. Many support teachers and applaud the leadership they provide.

Even the courts, despite what we hear about permissive judges and lenient sentencing, are helping:

August 29, 1984
PRISON POPULATION SOARING RECORD 454, 136 DOUBLE THAT OF A DECADE AGO (*Chicago Tribune*, 1984)

September 15, 1986
NATIONAL PRISON POPULATION RECORD 529,000 SAYS THE JUSTICE DEPARTMENT (*The Free Press*, 1986)

June 30, 1989
U.S.A. PRISON POPULATION HITS PEAK AT 673,567

What politician would rather spend money for incarceration than education? What parent wants his or her child to attend an unruly school? What judge does not understand the right every citizen has to live free from fear and intimidation? We need to help student teachers and teachers understand that they are needed now more than ever in our history. We need to help them understand that how they discipline today will determine the kind of life we will all enjoy, and we need to help them believe that the great majority supports them and their efforts.

Teachers know the problems only too well: two and a half million students are absent from public schools daily, and a significant percentage are truants who are likely to participate in unproductive, disruptive, or even criminal activities (NSSC, 1989). One in seven children are bullied or are bullies. One in four of these bullies will have a criminal record by the time they are 30 (NSSC, 1989). One in four children drop out of school, and out of all proportion, become welfare fathers, welfare mothers, and prison inmates.

We could go on and on: 600 gangs in Los Angeles; 700,000 attempted suicides each year; over a 100-percent increase in juvenile deaths due to homicide (Stewart, 1989); 1,500,000 juveniles arrested each year; and a 9,300-percent increase in juvenile arrests since the Depression era (Office of Juvenile Justice and Delinquency Prevention, 1984). Our country has problems and needs mature and responsible teachers.

We need to help student teachers understand that stopping the behavior of one or two children who keep other children from learning is the most important part of their job. It is so because the parents of the children being bothered have rights. They do not want immature, short-sighted, disruptive students to cheat their child out of an education. (And force them to work at the local fast-food outlet and live at home for the rest of their lives.) Caring parents cannot be in the classroom to keep their neighbor's child from interfering with their own child's right to learn. Because of this, we must make sure that these caring parents' rights are not violated. Schools are this country's major civilizing agency and should stand for morals as high as those in the best homes in America. Teachers should never lose sight of the good students who need encouragement to be good, nor of the good work done by parents that must be maintained by the schools.

We can also remind student teachers that when they are disciplining, they are modeling effective behaviors that can be used by students as they become adults.

Student teachers might also be taught that speaking out against public displays of antisocial behavior is proper and courageous and should be encouraged and reinforced. We should emphasize, however, that encouraging citizens to speak out when confronted with rude and boorish behavior requires walking a tight wire.

At a minimum, 5 percent of those people who honk or shake their fists at us when we do not move quickly enough at the stop light or cut into line at the theater or talk too loudly in the library do not function well around others and do not react in anticipated ways. Many have been in mental hospitals, are drunk, or are on "work-release programs." At at a minimum, 3 million people in our society have just been released from jail or prison or are on parole (N.I.J. Reports, 1990).

It would be wise for us to encourage student teachers and teachers to be prudent and to use common sense when confronting misbehavior. At times, it is anything but cowardly to run away or tell people that they are right, even though they are not, or even to get down on our knees and beg. All we need to do is read the newspaper to know that our free, democratic, pluralistic society includes many people who act out the urges that pop into their heads. Inaction is, of course, action, but sometimes inaction is appropriate.

As we stated earlier, discipline is a matter of attitude. But it also is a matter of seeing the big picture and doing what is best for the individual *and* society. Yet it is more; it is ignoring some administrators, some parents, some fellow teachers, and some advice. And it is finding the courage to act and to know when we have gone as far as we can go.

Student teachers need to know that society has entrusted them with discovering, teaching, and enforcing the standards and ideals necessary for our civilized society to survive. Teachers need to know that they can sense intuitively what is appropriate and what is not, what society can tolerate and what it cannot, and which actions on the part of students are cruel and deliberate and which are just thoughtless and accidental. Teachers need to trust their feelings and act upon them. A teacher's assessment of a student's behavior is still the best long-range predictor we have for determining whether a student will adjust socially or become delinquent.

As university supervisors, we should encourage student teachers to believe that their teaching is too important and their mission too vital to allow a few uncivilized, ill-mannered, and spoiled children to make them quit. We should encourage them to believe that they may become the best teacher in the world, and they should not allow anyone to rob those not yet born of such a teacher!

The above material is what we believe student teachers should learn during student teaching: to trust themselves, to discipline in ways that help students behave when teachers are not around, to put what is best for society first, and to see the bigger picture.

What follows are seven items of advice that we have heard cooperating teachers give student teachers. Our reactions to this advice are also included.

1. "The first thing you must learn is that students are going to test you because you are new. And then they are going to retest you to see if you can hang in there. You have to be stronger than they are."

REACTION: Welcome student criticism. If you can get a group that is open and will level with you, rejoice—they will make a teacher out of you.

Do not be overly concerned about being conned. It does not take long to separate the serious from those setting you up. Besides, if you are being made too big a fool, your students will rat on each other. That is one of the real joys of teaching—seeing students' fair play in action. Their sense of fair play far exceeds that of most adults.

2. "You will have behavior problems—the best do."

REACTION: As a graduate student, one of the authors recalls a professor telling him how the dropout rate for inner-city student teachers changed from 80 percent not completing the term to 80 percent completing the semester. This was accomplished by using role playing. A student, about to student teach, was asked to teach three adults for half an hour. These adults played the roles of students—they were rude, crude, disruptive, abusive, and disrespectful. Sometimes the student teachers cried and fled from the room, but they were always urged to continue.

Anticipating is the first step many cooperating teachers urge, because when you expect something, you are not caught off guard, and you are more apt to behave with sound judgment.

3. "Do not be a jerk in the lounge. Teaching is complicated. Do not start off by offending those who can help."

REACTION: We often wonder how a student teacher, challenged by a multitude of decisions, with a minimum of time to consider alternatives, and having no stockpile experience to draw upon, no frame of reference, gets the courage even to try. Nothing is more important for you than to develop a close relationship with your cooperating teacher and other teachers in the building.

4. "Disciplining students will take up much of your time. During my first year of teaching I made extensive lesson plans, but discipline took up so much of my time that I never got through them."

REACTION: True, a well-planned lesson does not stop all discipline problems, but a disorganized, unprepared teacher, instead of having problems, has chaos. Believe that what you are teaching is important, that it is necessary for your students to learn it, and that class time is too important to be wasted.

5. "Do not be a yeller and a screamer. They will just tune you out."

REACTION: This, of course, is true. But beyond that, yelling and screaming can be harmful. Yelling and screaming provide therapy for the teacher and amusement for the cutups, but it often terrorizes the quiet and timid. Quiet students are your greatest allies. If push comes to shove, and it becomes secret ballot time, they will be on your side. Do not alienate them. Their needs are as great as your troublemakers' needs. They just do not wear them on their sleeves. Teach the quiet ones how to become more assertive. And, by example, teach them ways they might react to similar problems in the outside world, such as late parties at public campgrounds, swearing on public buses, and loud talking in movie theaters. It is not written in stone that bullies and con artists will inherit the earth.

6. "If it is necessary for you to be labeled a tyrant, then let it be. Many student teachers want to be popular and become 'buddies' with students. I feel that it is more important to be respected at first."

REACTION: Also learn to say no. Ignore the hurt looks and "why nots," and just say no. It is much easier to change a "no" to a "yes" than vice versa. Being called Mr. and Ms., having others ask you for permission, being respected—this is pretty heavy stuff. But what is so easily given can be easily taken away. Student cliques can make or break a student teacher. The popular ones, the leaders, the "in" groups, can laugh at the misfit and make you laugh along, because if you do not, they can bring out their deadly stares, their cold shoulders, their vicious rumors, and the game playing that will quickly let you know who is *really* boss. It takes courage to stand up for those too weak to defend themselves; it takes courage to forego popularity and do the right and decent thing; and it takes courage to buck the system and to stop giving those who need the least help the most.

Train yourself to rely on sources other than popularity for a sense of well-being. Derive satisfaction from seeing students learn, from seeing the quiet become more outspoken, and from seeing the self-centered learn to care about others.

7. "I have watched student teachers in our department go through some pretty hard experiences. My suggestion to them would be to use the "assertive discipline' approach."

REACTION: Lee Canter's approach of writing a student's name on the board and making a check mark beside it if they misbehave works, because it spells out what a teacher will not tolerate, and because it encourages even the most timid teacher to act. Have high expectations. Be aware, however, that assertive discipline does little to change attitudes. Writing names on the board, making students stay after school, and rewarding their "good" behavior keeps them in check while in our classrooms, but does little to make them behave when we are not around.

Be suspicious of any quick fix. Try to find out what is behind behavior. Before you act quickly, ask yourself these three questions: Can the children I am about to discipline behave? Do they know the correct way to behave? Are they aware they are misbehaving?

Sometimes discipline is as simple as accepting what cannot be changed, teaching the correct ways to behave, and reminding students that they are out of line. Sometimes it is even more simple than that. Often children, like adults, "misbehave" if they have lost too much sleep or are hungry or cannot hear or cannot see. Punishment is always an option; why not first try understanding the reason they misbehave?

In closing, we have three bits of advice that university supervisors might share with student teachers:

1. When it comes to discipline, remember that there are no easy solutions and that not even seasoned veterans have all the answers. Teaching is the most complicated job in the world! Not everyone can teach at the elementary or secondary level. And the main reason

they cannot is that "little" thing called discipline.

Just do your best and do not allow your first group to be selfish beasts. You may teach for forty years. Do not let one group, your first, drive you out.

2. Resolve before you start student teaching that you do not deserve to be trampled upon; that you have something to offer others; and that you are a human being and deserve a fair chance.

3. Before your first day, remind yourself of the characteristics of a good boss—a person you would walk across the street to introduce to your parents. Do they respect you, listen to you, treat you as if you have a brain? Are they friendly toward you, accepting, caring, genuine, and fair?

Remember, you are your students' boss. What you like and admire in a boss they will like and admire in you.

Chapter 13

The University Supervisor and Curriculum

If university supervisors are to work effectively and credibly in host schools, they need to be knowledgeable in the field of curriculum. This is because they make curriculum decisions every day. Each time they critique a student teacher's lesson plans, or answer a question such as, "What is your opinion of outcome-based education?" they make a curriculum decision.

When supervisors observe a class and comment, "The filmstrip on Hemingway was excellent, and I am pleased that you pointed out it was more critical than most sources regarding his inability to develop female characters," or when they say, "I know you have been taught to speak almost entirely in German, Betty, but your first-year German students are not following you," they are making curriculum decisions.

University supervisors deal with subject matter curriculum, curriculum trends, spiral curriculum, and K–12 curriculum daily. They work with student teachers in different subject matter fields and see firsthand the interdisciplinary nature of curriculum.

They are surrounded by a multitude of opportunities for becoming involved in curriculum. So many, in fact, that we wonder why more members of university curriculum departments are not involved in supervision. Supervision provides the ultimate opportunity for putting curriculum theory into practice.

This chapter presents a rationale for university supervisors becoming involved in the study of curriculum and includes a look at the changing school curriculum, curriculum insights that university supervisors might offer host schools, guidelines for becoming involved with the school curriculum, student teachers' initial involvement with curriculum, and the need for credibility.

THE CHANGING SCHOOL CURRICULUM

The curriculum—the master plan of courses, activities, and programs that organize and promote the academic and extra-curricular activities of a school—dictates what subjects or courses are taught and, to a large degree, the grade level at which the subjects are offered. It is a guide indicating the sequence of course offerings, academic accomplishments expected, and eligibility requirements for class participants. At the elementary level especially, the curriculum may dictate the approach or methodology used.

The curriculum in most districts is now in a complete state of change. This change is ongoing and will continue until the needs of all children are met and all state mandates are accomplished—in other words, forever. Curricula nationwide have been influenced by a number of things, among them failing Scholastic Aptitude Test scores and poor achievement in science, mathematics, history, geography, and reading. In addition to declining test scores and poor achievement, curricula have been impacted by:

> increased attention to education in values; emphasis on drug, alcohol, and AIDS education; heated debate over earlier admission of children to schools; demands for the improved teaching of thinking skills and the improved learning of subject matter with which to think; and closer observation of what makes systems of education in foreign countries seem to succeed. (Doll, 1986, p. 17)

Add to these influences the implementation of new technology, including personal computers, television channels designed especially for the schools such as Channel One, microstorage of library materials on CD ROM (compact disc-read only memory), and we begin to comprehend the magnitude of the nationwide change occurring in our curriculum.

Curriculum change is also occurring at the state level. State legislators are tremendously interested in education. Sometimes they even pass laws requiring that certain subject matters be taught. Often, however, they simply appoint committees to make recommendations to them or create boards that act in their behalf. Most of the change at the state level comes from the state department of education. This is a group that "accredits and monitors school programs, disburses state and federal-through-state moneys for special programs, enforces standards for high school graduation, and sets specifications for amounts of time to be devoted to specific content areas" (Oliva, 1988, p. 86).

At the local level, the curriculum is also changing. Administrative personnel, namely superintendents and principals, are delegated authority by the local school board to develop the school curriculum. They are also responsible for meeting state requirements for graduation and standards necessary to qualify for special programs, funds, and grants. All of these activities, and especially how administrators *interpret* them, influence and change the curriculum. Teachers also generate curriculum change but only within established parameters.

CURRICULUM INSIGHTS UNIVERSITY SUPERVISORS MIGHT BRING TO HOST SCHOOLS

University supervisors generally work with more than one district. In doing so, they have an excellent opportunity to view curriculum development, implementation, and evaluation in a variety of situations and have a chance to observe how each school interprets its respective curriculum. They see how individual districts tailor their curriculum to meet special needs— for example, through magnet schools—and they see different strategies used to promote multicultural attitudes. They see the whole picture, the global effect, without being swayed by personal involvement.

There are at least seven areas in which university supervisors might offer curriculum insights: class format, teaching strategies, grouping, current materials, classroom management, grading and evaluation strategies, and new printed material (Wiles & Bondi, 1989).

First, university supervisors have numerous occasions to observe the class format. They are present in classes where team teaching provides students with excellent learning experiences and where personalities of teachers model skills being taught. They observe cooperation in action, teamwork by teachers, sharing of responsibilities, and differences in opinion handled in a positive manner. University supervisors see the merits and disadvantages of short and long class periods, lengthened school days, and flexible scheduling. When shared these insights can profit both student and cooperating teachers.

A second area of input is teaching strategies. As observers in classrooms containing students from all types of social, environmental, and psychological backgrounds, university supervisors take note of the success of teaching strategies used in a variety of situations. More important, they observe teachers modifying teaching strategies to fit particular situations.

Grouping of students is the third area in which the university supervisor can share experience and knowledge. Working with a number of districts provides an opportunity to study the merits of large and small groups, heterogeneous versus homogeneous classes, graded versus ungraded groups, one teacher per class versus team teaching, and scheduling priorities for the gifted.

A fourth area in which university supervisors might share insights is contemporary technology (e.g., audio and video tapes, public television programming, special television programs suitable for classroom viewing, and computer hardware and software). By being in a variety of classrooms, university supervisors have an opportunity to become knowledgeable and can share this knowledge with student teachers and cooperating teachers. That sharing might include the sources, availability, approximate cost of the materials, and especially the name of a person to contact for more information.

Classroom management is a fifth area in which supervisors can offer expertise. Cooperating teachers have developed their own strategies through experience, class personality, school policy, and the need to survive each day. In helping student teachers develop classroom management skills best suited to their teaching style and personality, university supervisors need to work closely with cooperating teachers who understand local school policy and who can explain why current management strategies are being used.

The sixth area is grading and evaluation strategies. University supervisors observe and evaluate a variety of strategies for recording student progress. In sharing this experience and knowledge, they can aid student teachers in developing alternative strategies for evaluating students and can help them think through school policy regarding both grading and recording.

A final area in which university supervisors can share is new printed material. This could be in the form of new texts or new teaching programs in subjects such as math, language arts, science, and reading. Again, university supervisors see new materials presented at conferences or on campus, and they receive complimentary texts in advance and observe new programs presented in host schools. All of this information can be shared.

An often overlooked way of helping host schools in the area of curriculum is asking foreign students attending the university to speak at host schools. Most are top students and are eager to share information about their country, customs, and general way of life.

GUIDELINES FOR BECOMING INVOLVED WITH THE SCHOOL CURRICULUM

It is imperative that university supervisors become familiar with the curriculum requirements of each host school and, if possible, the external and internal forces that caused the curriculum to evolve as it did. For some districts, the curriculum is law; for others, it is a guide. And in some districts, what students want to study becomes the curriculum. One of the best ways to gain knowledge about the curriculum is to approach administrators, curriculum directors, and cooperating teachers with such questions as: "What do I need to know about your curriculum to do a better job of supervising student teachers?" "What is the reason you chose Scott Foresman for your reading program and McGraw-Hill for mathematics?" "I have just read the state School Board Association's summary of the education bill passed by the Senate. If the governor signs it, could we meet next week to discuss its impact upon your curriculum?" Other questions that might be appropriate are: "What should our student teachers know about your curriculum?" "Would it be possible for our student teachers to attend your curriculum workshops?" "What effect is this second year of using site-based management having upon your curriculum?"

University supervisors need to be tactful and to tread lightly when involved in host-school curriculum matters. Cooperating teachers and school administrators may like their curriculum as it is! They may judge their curriculum to be excellent because their students score high on SAT tests, their graduates have a fine record in advance placement in colleges of their choice, and their graduates have been successful in completing college or other post-high-school programs.

When working with other professionals, university supervisors should not jump to conclusions or make value judgments until all the facts are known. Occasionally, teachers are expected to use and teach from texts that they did not order and do not like. It is also possible that a particular portion of the curriculum that you may be criticizing is one the cooperating teacher had a part in developing. Teachers have the privilege of criticizing that for which they are responsible. Guests do not.

If, however, a legitimate and professional request is made for you to evaluate the curriculum, accept this leadership role if you feel qualified.

The guiding principle for all supervisors to remember is that they are guests in the school. The school has been operating prior to their arrival and will continue to operate after they leave. As guests, their function does not generally include transforming the existing curriculum. Their function as supervisors is to help student teachers understand why the curriculum is like it is, to help student teachers understand how they might change the curriculum once they become full-time teachers, and to help student teachers do the best job possible in spite of feelings about the present curriculum.

STUDENT TEACHERS' INITIAL INVOLVEMENT WITH THE CURRICULUM

Most school districts selected as host schools for student teachers are accredited. They have a curriculum that meets requirements identified by the accrediting agency in addition to those imposed by the state and federal governments. The host district may increase requirements already imposed regarding academic achievement, courses offered, and graduation requirements. Since resulting curriculum may differ from district to district, it would be prudent for university supervisors and directors of student teaching programs to be aware of differences between available programs so that the needs of student teachers might best be met.

Student teachers need to be aware of the curriculum in schools where they are student teaching. It helps them in planning their lessons if they have a general idea of what students have been taught and will study in the future. For example, a student teacher who has been assigned to teach seventh-grade mathematics should be aware of units that have been taught previously. A student teacher assigned to a ninth-grade social studies class should be aware of what the social studies curriculum has provided for students during their first eight years and what it will provide in grades ten through twelve. If assigned to teach fourth-grade reading, the student teacher should be aware of the reading proficiency level expected for students entering that grade. Student teachers need to know such things before they can establish reasonable objectives and outcomes for units they will be preparing.

THE NEED FOR CREDIBILITY

When university supervisors work with cooperating teachers, curriculum directors, administrators, and student teachers, they must be aware of the impact that decisions involving curriculum have upon students. The rules under which the curriculum is established, functions, and dictates to its clientele are unique to that particular elementary or secondary school; criticism is not usually taken lightly. University supervisors who have worked with the same school districts for several years have had the time and opportunity to build trust, rapport, and understanding. They have established credibility and may be called on for advice, counsel, and input into matters dealing with curriculum.

Credibility in a host school is earned. Credibility is not given lightly; it is possible to have credibility with one or more teachers but not all. Credibility is gained through serving. Service to the host schools is a bridge, whether it is judging a science fair, speech, or debate tournament; speaking at a local service club; or working with an in-service group to plan for future learning opportunities with the local district. Once credibility has been established, the opportunities to become involved in local curriculum evaluation, development, and implementation are greatly enhanced. It must be remembered, however, that credibility can be lost much more easily than it was gained.

As confidence in university supervisors develops, so will credibility with the staff and administration of the host school. University supervisors may be asked to help plan and possibly be involved with staff development. This might be through special presentations for specific groups of teachers, presentations to the entire staff, working with mentoring programs for new staff, or curriculum evaluation followed by curriculum development. Many university supervisors have been asked to participate in workshops, speak at in-service sessions, and make presentations at state and national conferences. Through attendance and participation at many different levels, they have opportunities to share their insight and knowledge with administrators and teachers at the local level.

One of the most appropriate ways of establishing credibility is through working with student teachers. The positive relationship that develops between cooperating teachers and university supervisors is an excellent vehicle for shared learning. Student teachers are in the process of transferring theory into practice. As the triad shares teaching philosophy, subject matter material, methodology, strategies for classroom management, and how all of these fit into the existing curriculum, a feeling of trust bonds them together. The curriculum of the school today is in a state of constant flux. Supervisors of student teachers, with the classroom experience, expertise in specific disciplines, ability to communicate, and willingness to serve, are a valuable resource to any host school.

In conclusion, university supervisors can be an important resource for any host school if: 1. They are knowledgeable about the field of curriculum in regard to evaluation, development, and implementation; 2. They have the poise, confidence, and common-sense skills to use their knowledge to help student teachers gain a working understanding of the curriculum content and how it functions; 3. They serve as liaison and resource persons whose skills are self-evident; and 4. Their first responsibility is to helping student teachers develop into the best teachers possible.

Beginning university supervisors may find the following readings useful: Johnson's (1967) "Definitions and Models in Curriculum Theory"; Taba's (1962) *Curriculum Development, Theory and Practice*; and Wiles and Bondi's (1989) *Curriculum Development: A Guide to Practice*.

Common Concerns of University Supervisors and Cooperating Teachers

This chapter addresses the concerns that experienced university supervisors, new university supervisors, and veteran cooperating teachers have regarding their role in the student teaching process.

EXPERIENCED UNIVERSITY SUPERVISORS' CONCERNS

A major concern of experienced university supervisors is the policy of student teacher placement. Some have limited or no input in this area. Frequently, student teachers' credentials are mailed to a school, and an official assigns them a cooperating teacher, using such criteria as the number of years the cooperating teacher has been in the system, the desire of the cooperating teacher to work with a student teacher, the student teacher's own request, and whether the cooperating teacher has earned a master's degree (Reitzammer, 1991). Assignment is often made with little regard for matching the strengths, personalities, and special needs of the student teacher with those of the cooperating teacher, and it is made with little or no input from the university supervisor. Some university supervisors never meet their assigned student teachers until the day before they begin student teaching, and the only information they receive beforehand is the student teacher's application.

A second concern of experienced university supervisors is departmental support. University supervisors often question if anyone really cares about what happens to student teachers once they leave campus. They also question whether the department will budget adequate funds to support travel to host schools. They even question if existing funds will be quietly transferred from the student teaching budget into programs that are more visible.

A third concern of veteran university supervisors is how they are perceived by members of their department, college, and the university at large. Some wonder if they are considered full-time professionals with all the rights, privileges, and status that goes with such a position. They wonder if their application for promotion and tenure will receive the same serious considerations as others in the university family. And they wonder how detrimental it will be to their chances of promotion and tenure that their need to be in host schools has kept them from serving on influential university committees.

A fourth concern of university supervisors is that they often feel no consideration is given to distances that they have to travel when the director of student teaching places student teachers. They ask themselves, "How can I spend an appropriate amount of time with my student teachers when I have to spend two hours just getting there?"

Such concerns as policies concerning placement, assignment of cooperating teachers, departmental support, how they are perceived by their peers, and consideration for distances traveled are real. They affect the work climate and the efficiency of those involved in supervision. Too often, these concerns are not addressed. They need to be discussed by the department each term.

In terms of placement policy and selection of cooperating teachers, we believe that university supervisors should place their own student teachers and meet them prior to placement. This way the best match possible between the student teacher and the cooperating teacher can be made. This assumes, however, that the university supervisor would work with the same schools for several years.

In terms of departmental support and how university supervisors are perceived by peers, we believe that they are not accepted as first-class citizens by some senior department members and administrators. Having said this, let us add that an individual gets about as much respect as he or she demands, *and* his or her sense of professionalism and self-confidence communicates itself. University supervisors have no reason whatsoever to feel their job is any more or any less important than anyone else's at the university.

And finally, in terms of the distance university supervisors drive to get to their work, we believe that many professors travel these days, and traveling has become part of being a university teacher. The disparity comes when one supervisor works near campus and has twenty student teachers and one works 100 miles from campus and also has twenty student teachers. This is clearly unfair, but unless the supervisor near campus is willing to accept twenty-five student teachers while the one who works further out in the field only has fifteen, there will probably not be much progress made. Such injustice is the reality surrounding how faculty positions are funded at many institutions.

CONCERNS OF ADJUNCT AND NEW UNIVERSITY SUPERVISORS

One of the first concerns of new university supervisors is the logistics of the position, that is, where they are assigned and where their schools are located. They are also concerned about the inevitable paper trail of forms, the requisitioning of vehicles, the cooperation they will receive at schools. Such concerns are normal and will disappear quickly. Supervision, like any new job, is a living hell the first two weeks.

A second concern of new or adjunct supervisors involves dealing with people during the initial contact. There are many introductions to be made, first impressions to worry about, and local traditions and policies of which to become aware. A recurring question from a new university supervisor is, "When I go to my schools for the initial visit, who do I see first?" Most host schools have a chain of command, and a new university supervisor, when in doubt, should start at the top of that chain. Most university supervisors, however, report to the principal's office immediately upon entering the building.

A third concern of new university supervisors is that they have generally received little or no formal training in how to supervise. The fact that few institutions offer advanced degrees in clinical supervision may be indicative of how some perceive the role of a supervisor. Hopefully, this book may help.

A fourth concern of new supervisors is finding sources of information on supervision. New university supervisors who look for ideas on how to supervise will find little in the way of printed help. There is a wide variety of information available for student teachers and for cooperating teachers but little for university supervisors. Few periodicals feature articles relating to university supervision, and there are few graduate programs that emphasize clinical supervision. Again, we hope this text may help.

A fifth concern of new supervisors is their place in the academic and social structure of the university. They have the same concerns regarding promotion, tenure, and faculty status as experienced supervisors. Those who are resident coordinators in student teaching centers (located away from campus) face an even more acute problem. Our advice is to talk to veteran supervisors. In this area, you are all on very common ground.

A sixth concern expressed by new supervisors is their ability to relate. They ask, "How do I relate to a college student? I've been working with elementary and secondary students for years, what will I find different about working with college seniors?" "How do I communicate and work with adults who are used to the freedom of the university?" "How do I avoid being pompous and overbearing, and how do I keep from treating college seniors like high-school students?"

Many of the questions, frustrations, and concerns of new university supervisors can be alleviated or reduced by a mentoring program for new university supervisors. (A mentoring program for university supervisors is discussed in Chapter 3.) Included in such a mentoring program would be frequent meetings where new and veteran supervisors could share experiences and knowledge.

COMMON CONCERNS OF VETERAN COOPERATING TEACHERS

Possibly the most common concern of veteran cooperating teachers is related to the big picture regarding the student teacher to whom they have been assigned. (All of Chapter 11 concerns working with first-year cooperating teachers.) "What kind of person will I be working with?" they ask. "I have read the information supplied by the university but it is pretty generic—an autobiography and a list of the classes in their major and minor fields. I want to know the *kind* of person I'm getting."

This concern may be remedied somewhat by a process in which student teachers are interviewed by the host school and departmental personnel prior to their acceptance. This process extends the time required for placement, but it is time more than compensated for by the feeling of ownership that host school personnel gain in the student teaching process.

A second concern of veteran cooperating teachers is the skill level in pedagogy and the knowledge level in subject matter that their untried and untested student teacher brings to the assignment. Cooperating teachers ask all sorts of questions: "Does my student teacher have any experience with our reading series?" "Will my student teacher, who has a broad background in social studies, be able to handle a unit on Latin American geography?" "Will they be able to relate to my below-average classes?" "Will they be able to understand student questions, motivate the slower ones, and teach at the students' level of comprehension?"

A third concern is whether student teachers can relate to students. "Will my student teacher remember what it was like to be gangly, have braces, and be clumsy?" "Will they remember what it was like to be a boy in the middle school—pimples, hormones out of control, trying to be 'cool', just trying to survive puberty let alone learning much?" "When I have just begun to get this class moving and working cooperatively, and am just now getting them to make progress, will my student teacher be able to continue this or will I have to start all over again when my student teacher leaves?"

A fourth concern of cooperating teachers regards the university supervisor. They say to us, "Who will the university supervisor be next term? We just get used to one and their style of operation, and then the university replaces them with another. I feel we are being used to train student teachers *and* university supervisors." All too often, this complaint is justified.

A final concern deals with the personalities of student teachers. We have heard cooperating teachers say the following: "What can we expect from this student teacher? The last one never visited the teachers' lounge, never attended staff meetings or teacher in-services. I got the impression that he was more of an aid than a student teacher. I want someone who is interested in teaching, involved and professional. I would not waste my time with the others."

But we have also heard cooperating teachers say: "Last year, two student teachers took over the teachers' lounge and acted as though it were the university student union. They were loud, boisterous, and, most of all, critical of our school. They made *us* feel like outsiders. Our problem is that we took it. But no more!"

The foremost thing that university supervisors need to be concerned about is taking the concerns of cooperating teachers seriously. Openness, honesty, and candor are almost always appreciated and welcomed by experienced, front-line cooperating teachers.

Close relationships must be built between university supervisors and cooperating teachers. Each needs to learn to depend on the other for feedback regarding the progress of their student teacher. Each needs to operate as a team member, sharing the expertise necessary to ensure a successful student teaching experience.

Many individuals like things planned in advance, specifics identified, and few exceptions made to the rules. Such people should probably avoid working with student teachers. What is needed when working with student teachers is flexibility, understanding, and a degree of empathy for those who are about to make mistakes. Those who work with student teachers need to know that their protégés are in the process of learning the profession and, as such, will make errors in judgment and mistakes in management, and will even fail to use suggestions offered by cooperating teachers and university supervisors. University supervisors and cooperating teachers need to recall their own student teaching experiences and keep in mind the frustrations, overreactions, and even the regrettable things that happened.

SUMMARY

You want what is best for our profession and our society; because of this you will always have concerns. Be thankful for them. They mean that you care and have not become indifferent. The one concern that you should never have, however, is that the role of the university supervisor will pass from existence. This has been talked about for years, there is talk about it now (Kagan, 1991), and there will be talk of it in the future. But it will not occur, because when vital educational issues are at stake and vital parts of the process of educating teachers are in jeopardy, reason rapidly surfaces and prevails. Teacher educators are a straight-thinking group. They have all student taught. Each knows that it takes extraordinary caring and special handling to help an insecure novice develop into a confident professional.

Chapter 15 _____

The Conflict between Individuality and Conformity

A chapter of this nature has been included because student teachers are forced immediately to decide whether to toe the line, go with the flow, and say what others want to hear, or whether to speak their mind, live their personal beliefs, and be their own person. From the beginning, they face the dilemma of deciding how much they are willing to conform in order to survive and graduate.

It is a difficult decision because student teachers know, at least in broad terms, what behaviors they would like to model and what values they would like to teach. They worry, however, that their cooperating teacher will not accept what they teach and how they teach it.

Student teachers, having recently been exposed to ideals in college, possess a keen sense of the kind of citizens that they feel our society needs. They want to produce persons who are independent in their thinking; who pursue their own excellence; who speak clearly, effectively, precisely, and fearlessly to the point; who question preconceptions; who have a love for knowledge and find happiness in the pursuit of knowing; who are devoid of vanity, greed, and malice; and who are citizens of good will, able and disposed to put themselves at the service of others. But again, they worry that those evaluating them may find their goals too lofty, their zest too threatening, and their rhetoric too impractical.

Student teachers are certain that if they can keep from betraying their sense of justice and can make the right decision at the right moment, they can positively affect the common good. And they see many things in need of changing.

They see that sexism and racism still exist and, in fact, may be escalating. They see our society treating atheists and others who pursue their own brand of truth unjustly. They see some being so homophobic that they form hate groups and engage in hate crimes. They see incidents of bigoted violence and crimes motivated by racial, ethnic, or sexual prejudice increasing; they see the activity of the Klu Klux Klan and the White Aryan Resistance escalating; and they see injustice directed against those who struggle for their share of humanity on the rise.

At the same time that student teachers ponder the issue of what needs to be changed and how they might accomplish this change, they see students shouting down other students on, of all things, a college campus. (In 1991, a Georgetown University student was shouted down by his peers when he tried to disclose that black students were being admitted to the law school with lower entrance scores than were accepted from white students.) They see college students rioting during spring break. And they see begging getting out of control. (In Washington, D.C., gangs of young men now bang on cars and demand money from the drivers.) They ask themselves, "Could the populace have mistakenly interpreted the freedoms guaranteed by our Constitution and Bill of Rights?"

Student teachers want to change society for the better. That is why they have become teachers. They want to judge students by what they do, not by who their parents are; they want to provide an opportunity for each student to be the best they can be; and they want to free the human mind and encourage trust in reason and follow truth wherever it may lead. But will they be given a chance? They sense that things may have already gotten too far out of hand and ask if anyone else senses the urgency for needed change. Are their goals unrealistic? Are their concerns too idealistic? Do their goals and concerns differ from ours when we student taught?

Student teachers are often confused by the cynicism that they encounter and by the lack of tolerance given to freedom of thought. They wonder, too, whether their host school really wants its students to comprehend the degree to which they have been limited by having grown up in only one specific culture? They ask, "Does my school genuinely want to nurture the expression of individual uniqueness? Does it want students to feel free to reject the tastes and habits of society? Does it really wish to encourage free thinkers, tolerance for diversity, and an absolute freedom of opinions? Does it wish to produce creative creators that make a world for themselves? How far can I go toward developing the unique qualities of an individual?" Our job is to help student teachers come to terms with their questions, to encourage them to ask even more questions, and to assure them that we respect their intelligence and their belief that the entire goal of education is to make a difference.

In addition to professional questions, student teachers often ask personal questions: "If a teacher's behavior does not hurt anyone and if a teacher does not use force on anyone, shouldn't their personal life be private—even if others may think their behavior foolish or wrong or even perverse? Shouldn't what they do with another consenting adult be their own business?" Here again, we can help them resolve their conflict between conformity and individuality by prompting them to accept responsibility for their own behavior and by informing them that deep thinkers and gifted persons have always seen life differently and have often felt out of sync with the majority.

Student teachers are also very concerned about how far they can go with their opinions. If they believe that competition is simply a system that allows one group to enrich itself by ruining others, dare they share this view? Or if they believe that the super-rich are immoral and should renounce their surplus in favor of those without, should they say this aloud? Or if they believe that the school in which they are now working is over-institutionalized, should they express this belief?

We can and should help student teachers with these dilemmas

by being their sounding board. If they can hear their beliefs uttered aloud without judgments being made, they can sort the wheat from the chaff, separate the important from the insignificant, and arrive at a reasoned position.

Student teachers do not want to be labeled by solid and established educators as difficult, but they do not want to be controlled like robots or treated as mindless persons either. They need help in overcoming their fear of disapproval and in discovering what risks are necessary to effect genuine change.

A little of our counsel at the right time can be immensely valuable in helping them adjust to the idea that by cooperating, they are not necessarily selling out to or being manipulated by the system.

There is truly no right or wrong way to supervise student teachers as long as what is best for the student teacher, the children being taught, and the society in which we live have been foremost in our minds. Student teachers are a hope for change. They come to us in an unspoiled state. We should encourage their idealism and support their desire to do the right thing.

We cannot overemphasize the skill that is necessary to help a rapidly changing novice become a professional. To survive as university supervisors, we need to be flexible and careful listeners, especially to what is not being said.

Can teachers who live and teach in a democracy be best prepared in an atmosphere of conformity to requirements imposed from above? Can they best be prepared to teach in our pluralistic society in an environment of uniformity, in which they are expected to echo the words of others and accept, without criticism, what they are told? Or can we best prepare student teachers, best help society, and best help the students that they will, in turn, teach by liberating the power within student teachers and by allowing them to show the many ways in which they are superior?

We need to help student teachers avoid being abrasive. We need to help them learn to handle sensitive individuals, and we need to encourage them to stimulate their students' ambition, to arouse their students' interest, and to encourage cooperation. Being a university supervisor is a superhuman assignment, a task that often causes us to feel pitifully and inadequately prepared. But if we can respect our student teachers and not act as judge *and* jury regarding their personal beliefs, and if we can assist them in expressing their opinions in productive ways, we can help them successfully walk that tight-wire between doing their own thing and doing what is best for themselves, their students, and society. A few words directed at them about their own special needs often helps more than a number of required courses.

The Present Status of and Future Trends in Supervision

Policies concerning student teaching placements, credit, grading, seminars, and the number of weeks of student teaching—as well as the roles and responsibilities of university supervisors—vary among the over 1,400 teacher-preparing institutions in the United States. What follows is a brief description of three programs of supervision and a summary of the present status of and future trends in supervision.

THREE PROGRAMS OF SUPERVISION

Mankato State University

As one of seven universities of the Minnesota State University System (MSUS), Mankato State in south central Minnesota is a comprehensive public university with more than 600 faculty and 16,000 students. MSU was established in 1868 as the second state normal school, became Mankato State Teachers College in 1921, was renamed Mankato State College in 1957, and gained university status in 1975. The university offers undergraduate and graduate degrees in education (B.S., M.S., M.A., M.A.T., and the specialist).

The College of Education houses seven resource programs and
ten departments, including the Department of Curriculum and
Instruction (C&I). Student teaching is under the direction of C&I.
The director of student teaching interviews and places student
teachers in rural, suburban, and urban school districts within
an approximate eighty-mile radius. Eligible students may participate in the MSUS Common Market, which allows them to
teach anywhere in the state or abroad. The director also assigns
student teachers to supervisors.

Student teachers teach during the fall, winter, or spring quarters of their senior year for ten weeks. They receive a pass/fail
grade and sixteen quarter-hours of credit.

University supervisors are responsible for providing an orientation (first seminar); conducting at least three additional seminars; supervising on a regular basis; writing final evaluations;
and determining whether the student teacher has passed or
failed. Cooperating teachers also submit final evaluations.

MSU utilizes full-time supervisors, part-time adjunct supervisors, and full-time faculty who supervise only as a part of their
load. Full-time supervisors, who are C&I faculty, supervise a
maximum of twenty student teachers per quarter. No specialists
are used, but special-methods faculty are invited to accompany
generalists if they wish.

St. Olaf College

St. Olaf College in Northfield, Minnesota, is a four-year private liberal-arts college affiliated with the Evangelical Lutheran
Church. It has over 200 faculty, with 3,000 students. The teacher
education program is primarily secondary with the exception of
K–12 programs in art, music, and physical education. Student
teachers complete student teaching in the fall or spring semesters
of their senior year. An increasing number of students, however,
are returning as ninth-semester student teachers. Students receive 2.5 course credits (9.12 semester hours) for student teaching. All student teachers teach from ten to fourteen weeks.
Placements are made within a sixty-mile radius of the campus
in rural, suburban, and urban school districts. Even though students choose where they want to student teach, most placements

tend to be concentrated in nearby towns and suburbs. A limited number may participate in student teaching programs in Chicago, Texas, and abroad.

The director of student teaching and certification is responsible for interviewing students regarding their placement, making the placements, scheduling visits for both generalists and specialists, conducting student teaching orientation sessions, scheduling and conducting seminars, conducting exit conferences, grading student teachers, and processing licensure requests for alumni. The director also supervises student teachers and teaches two courses.

All student teachers are supervised by a Department of Education supervisor (often called a generalist) and a special methods supervisor (often called a specialist). The education supervisor makes three or more scheduled visits, and the specialist generally makes two. Most supervisors, both generalists and specialists, are full-time faculty with teaching loads. Supervising six student teachers is one course equivalent in a six-course FTE system. To accommodate an increasing number of teacher candidates in recent years, adjunct faculty have been hired as generalists to supervise on a part-time basis.

Generalists are responsible for orienting cooperating teachers to the student teaching program. This is done informally during the first visit to the school.

All student teachers are brought back to campus for three two-hour seminars each semester. Only generalists are present at these seminars. Generalists and specialists, as well as cooperating teachers, write separate formal evaluations at the end of the term. All evaluations are placed in the student teacher's permanent credential file. Both generalists and specialists recommend a letter grade for each student teacher to the director of student teaching who makes the final decision in assigning a grade.

University of Northern Iowa

The University of Northern Iowa (UNI) in Cedar Falls is a public comprehensive university with over 800 faculty and 12,000 students. It was established in 1876 as the Iowa State

Normal School. Its mission remains unchanged as evidenced by a recent undergraduate catalog statement: "It provides leadership in the development of programs for the pre-service and in-service preparation of teachers and other educational personnel for schools, colleges, and universities." UNI offers undergraduate and graduate degrees in education, including the specialist and doctorate.

The College of Education includes seven instructional units and the Office of Student Field Experiences (OSFE). The coordinator of OSFE is responsible for administering the student teaching component and other undergraduate teacher-education-program field experiences.

Student teachers receive twelve semester hours of credit for student teaching. All student teachers teach for sixteen weeks with two eight-week assignments. They choose a site from existing student teaching centers, including the Malcolm Price Laboratory School or overseas in U.S.-style schools.

Ten student teaching centers are geographically dispersed throughout the state in urban, suburban, and rural school systems. Each center is staffed with a resident coordinator (professor/coordinator of student teachers) who is a UNI faculty member. The coordinator is responsible for student teacher orientations, placement, weekly seminars, supervision of student teachers, final evaluations, and grades. The coordinator collaborates with center administrators, cooperating teachers, a Teaching Associates Cadre, and clinical supervisors.

The clinical supervisor is a local school district employee within a student teaching center and holds a one-half-time position funded by UNI. The clinical supervisor's major responsibility is to provide classroom supervision for UNI student teachers. Clinical supervisors assist the resident coordinator/professor with the selection of cooperating teachers and the placement, seminars, and evaluation of student teachers. They also work with the Teaching Associates Cadre on special projects.

The Teaching Associates Cadre is a network of public school educators tied to UNI's ten off-campus student teaching centers. Each of the ten cadres is connected to UNI through cadre members' direct involvement with the College of Education. Cadre members are "master educators" who participate in UNI-sponsored on-campus cadre conferences on program improvement and in off-campus activities such as assisting UNI faculty train and upgrade the supervisory skills of cooperating teachers.

Many of the program characteristics described in these three examples are representative of other student teaching programs across the nation.

THE PRESENT STATUS OF SUPERVISION

In a recent national survey on the "Role and Responsibilities of Directors of Field Experiences," Owings and Reitzammer (1991) found, among other things, that of 1,124 American colleges and universities:

> 96% + place students off-campus for student teaching; student teaching is a full-time experience at 90% + institutions; most internships (56.5%) last 10, 12 or 14 weeks; student teachers spend 7 or 8 hours per day in the internship at about 75% of the institutions; the final grade in student teaching is largely determined by the college supervisor; over 50% had less than eight college supervisors; 46.5% reported that supervising five or six student teachers was equivalent to teaching one course; over 60% required four, five or six evaluations by the college supervisor; 57.1% required two, three or four evaluations by the cooperating teacher; 50.9% conducted small seminars in training cooperating teachers; and 55.7% assign letter grades [A,B,C, etc.,] for student teaching. (p. 1–2)

These statistics yield significant information on what is currently happening with student teaching programs. However, it is important to note that these statistics do not take into account the type or model of student teaching program being implemented.

MacNaughton, Johns, and Rogus (1978) have identified five models that illustrate how the roles and responsibilities of university supervisors and classroom teacher educators vary. They base these models upon a literature review and input from consultants in state and private teacher-preparing institutions (p. 20). The model name (which actually classifies classroom teacher educators) and the role of university supervisors as described by MacNaughton and others are as follows:

The Traditional Model: The university supervisor . . . observes student performance, consults with the classroom teacher educator(s), provides support assistance to students, and formally assesses student effectiveness in relation to program objectives.

The Modified Traditional Model: The likelihood of supervisor involvement in inservice with teaching staff and curriculum development activity is enhanced over the traditional. Also student observations are likely to be of greater frequency since less school-to-school travel is required. Clustering may lead to the university supervisor's assuming an administrative and facilitative role. The concentration of students permits the university to appoint one on-site supervisor who, in addition to providing on-site supervision, makes placements, coordinates field work, gathers evaluations, and manages in-service programs. Also the model allows the supervisor more time to spend in the schools working with children in the classroom setting.

The Clinical Professor Model: The university supervisor and classroom teacher educator are one. This individual works with pre-student teachers, student teachers, and practicing teachers and may also coordinate teacher in-service activities on site. [Such as a laboratory school teacher.]

The Teacher Adjunct Model: The university supervisor's role is to maintain close contact with the classroom teacher educator, but he/she does not generally supervise the pre-student teachers or student teachers. The university supervisor provides liaison and program coordinating services, including curriculum development and in-service assistance.

Master Teacher-Apprentice Model: The role of the university supervisor does not exist since only the grade recording function needs to be carried out. (p. 20–25)

The Mankato State University and St. Olaf College programs described earlier could be classified as "traditional." The UNI program could be classified as a "modified traditional model." Some universities with laboratory schools utilize the "clinical professor model."

By and large, the last two models as described above significantly alter the university supervisor's role and responsibilities. One must seriously weigh the extent to which classroom teacher educators outside of a campus school setting should be given autonomy and be held solely responsible for supervising student teachers. Reasons for such caution are: the student teacher is a student of the university and of the teacher preparation program; many classroom teacher educators are not prepared for their role as supervisor; and many classroom teachers feel overworked already and do not want the additional responsibility. But the most important reason for caution is that the student teacher deserves to be evaluated by an objective, experienced, outside mediator who understands student teachers.

It is unknown how many institutions subscribe to nontraditional programs of supervision. Due to reform in teacher education, new approaches are frequently being discussed and developed. For example, the Holmes Group (1986) recommends that professional preparation for teaching begin after the baccalaureate degree is earned. In this model, students complete an internship (student teaching) during the fifth year while simultaneously enrolled in professional education courses. University supervisors' roles in fifth-year programs vary. In some programs, they are nonexistent because classroom teacher educators, serving as mentors, assume most of the responsibility for supervision. It is envisioned, however, that in these programs, the university supervisor would assume new responsibilities, much like those assumed by a doctor working with interns in a clinical setting.

Regardless of the current trends in supervision and the roles that university supervisors will play in the future, one thing is certain—the need for well-prepared supervisors is paramount. The preparation of university supervisors is a critical issue in developing effective student teaching programs, because the supervising role is complex and demanding. Niemeyer and Moon (1978) believe, as do the authors, that "supervision is not a linear activity, but involves reflection, introspection, intuition and an understanding of the dialectical nature of the role" (p. 6). "In theory and often in practice, the university supervisor is responsible for as many as fifty different and partially related tasks, teaching, evaluating and coordinating students and programs" (Nerenz, 1979, p. 471). To help develop effective teachers, supervisors must perform at least nine functions: leader, interpreter, observer, counselor, analyst, evaluator, facilitator, clinician, and humanitarian. (Jones, 1970) In light of these complex responsibilities and functions, it is imperative that only well-prepared teacher educators be allowed to supervise.

FUTURE TRENDS IN SUPERVISION

We cannot say what supervision will be like in the future, but we can make predictions. Currently, debate over maintaining undergraduate teacher preparation programs versus developing fifth-year programs continues. Some teacher educators would like to see all teachers prepared under the Holmes Group fifth-year model. Others would prefer to see traditional or modified traditional models used to prepare teachers.

There are several major issues involved in this debate. One issue is that of choice. Do we give all students who want to be teachers a chance to prove that they can be? Or do we only allow a selected few to become teachers? To date, many of those universities implementing fifth-year programs are large research-based institutions that have increased admissions standards and capped teacher candidate enrollments. Many state universities and smaller public and private colleges maintaining undergraduate teacher education programs have also increased admissions standards but have not limited enrollments.

A second issue is cost. Most financial aid for students ends with attainment of the baccalaureate degree. Thus, the expense of a fifth year at many private institutions would be prohibitive, and, consequently, sound programs would be ultimately and needlessly destroyed.

A third issue is financial incentives. Are teacher salaries high enough to attract those who have invested over five years in higher education? (Many fifth-year programs are actually longer than an academic year.) If not, from where will additional funds come to support needy students who want to become teachers? A fourth issue is graduate programs. Many smaller public and private colleges currently do not offer graduate degrees. College missions do not include graduate study, nor are funds available to implement such programs. Will these institutions, some of which are outstanding, be bypassed?

The last issue is that of data to support a fifth-year program over current undergraduate programs. Until such hard data is available, many four-year programs will continue in the current tradition until the issues described above are resolved.

In the future, the roles and responsibilities of university supervisors will most likely have many present-day characteristics. But supervisors undoubtedly will also be expected to increase their involvement with elementary or secondary schools and teachers (i.e., do more in-service work with faculty, demonstration teaching, etc.).

How will supervisors be prepared for future roles and responsibilities? In 1990 Scholl proposed:

A program of inservice should be developed and carried out to update the university supervisor's knowledge base, skills and application techniques as they relate to instructional supervision of the student teaching process and the on-going training of cooperating teachers as instructional supervisors. Without special preparation in supervision, it is unlikely that the university can provide the knowledge, leadership or influence that is necessary to supervise the complex experience of student teaching. (p. 4)

Not only do teacher educators suggest that university supervisors need special in-service training, but some, like Scholl, propose that supervisors be primarily responsible for training cooperating teachers (Horton & Harvey, 1979; Oja, 1988). Since cooperating teachers supervise student teachers on a daily basis, they, too, must be carefully prepared to supervise in a professional manner (MacNaughton, Jones, & Rogus, 1978). However, if university supervisors are going to be charged with formally preparing cooperating teachers, supervisors themselves must first have supervisory training.

Studies indicate that teacher educators desire in-service opportunities (Rush & Wood, 1982; Troyer, 1986; Uhlig & Haberman, 1987) but are limited by a "lack of available time, excessive work load, inadequate finances, inconvenient dates, and inappropriate content" (Troyer, 1986, p. 9). Administrators might consider reallocating funds to provide appropriate in-service for those who have no formal preparation in supervision and for experienced supervisors as well.

As the authors describe in Chapter 3, the documented need for the preparation of university supervisors, including the essential knowledge, skills, attitudes, and attributes, points to two recommendations. These recommendations are an internship and successful completion of a course designed especially for university supervisors on the supervision of student teachers.

The authors charge schools, colleges, and departments of education with acknowledging the following: that competent university supervisors are needed as much as competent professors in other academic areas and are needed as much as competent K–12 educators; that effective supervisors need certain knowledge and special skills, attitudes, attributes, and experiences; that measures must be taken to ensure that those faculty responsible for supervising student teachers are given in-service preparation on supervision; and that the future of education depends on a successful and well-supervised student teaching program.

University supervisors may find the following readings useful in identifying, sorting out, and developing an approach to supervision: Bennie's (1972) *Supervising Clinical Experiences in the Classroom*, Cogan's (1972) *Clinical Supervision*, Eisner's (1982) *An Artistic Approach to Supervision*, Goldhammer, Anderson, and Krajewski's (1980) *Clinical Supervision: Special Methods for the Supervision of Teachers*, McNeil's (1982) *A Scientific Approach to Supervision*, Raths and Leeper's (1966) *The Supervisor: Agent for Change in Teaching*, and Valverde's (1982) *The Self-Evolving Supervisor*.

Bibliography

Allen, D. W. (1966). Microteaching: A new framework for in-service education. *High School Journal, 49*, May, 355–363.

Allen, P. M. (1970). *Teacher self-appraisal: A way of looking over your own shoulders.* Worthington, OH: Charles A. Jones.

Allen-Hagen, B. (1991). Children in custody 1989. *National Institute of Justice Report, 223,* 20–21.

Alschuler, A. S. (1980). *School discipline, a socially literate solution.* New York: McGraw-Hill.

Amidon, E. J., and Flanders, N. A. (1971). *The role of the teacher in the classroom.* St. Paul, MN: Association for Productive Teaching.

Amidon, E. J., and Glammatteo, M. (1965). The verbal behavior of superior teachers. *Elementary School Journal, 65,* Spring, 283–285.

Association for Student Teaching. (1964). *The college supervisor—conflict and challenge—forty-third yearbook.* Dubuque, IA: William C. Brown.

Association for Student Teaching Yearbook. (1949). *The evaluation of student teaching.* Lockhaven, PA: Association of Student Teaching.

Bellack, A., and Davitz, J. (1966). *The language of the classroom.* New York: Teachers College Press.

Bennie, W. A. (1972). *Supervising clinical experiences in the classroom.* New York: Harper & Row.

Berger, S. T. (1983). *The developing person through the life span*. New York: Worth.

Berman, S. (1990). Educating for social responsibility. *Educational Leadership, 48* (3), 73–80.

Berne, E. (1964). *Games people play*. New York: Ballantine Books.

Blair, L., Curtis, D., and Moon, A. E. (1958). The purposes, function, and uniqueness of the college-controlled laboratory school. *Association of Student Teaching Bulletin #9*. Cedar Falls, IA: Association of Student Teaching.

Bloom, B. S. (1956). *Taxonomy of educational objectives, handbook I: Cognitive domain*. New York: David McKay.

Borich, G. D. (1977). *The appraisal of teaching: Concepts and processes*. Reading, MA: Addison-Wesley.

Bowman, N. (1978). Student teacher supervision, practices, and policies. *Action in Teacher Education, 1*, 64.

Brunner, C. E., and Majewski, W. S. (1990). Mildly handicapped students can succeed with learning styles. *Educational Leadership, 48* (2), 21–23.

Caine, R. N., and Caine, G. (1990). Understanding a brain-based approach to learning and teaching. *Educational Leadership, 48* (2), 66–70.

Canfield, A., and Canfield, J. S. (1986). *Canfield Instrumental Styles Inventory*. Ann Arbor, MI: Humanics Media.

Charles, C. M. (1989). *Building classroom discipline* (3rd edition). New York: Longman.

Chicago Tribune. (1984, August, 29). p. 1, sec. 1.

Claxton, C. S., and Murrell, P. H. (1987). *Learning styles: Their impact on teaching and administration*. AAHE–ERIC/Higher Education Research Report No. 10. Washington, D.C.: American Association for Higher Education.

Cogan, M. L. (1972). *Clinical supervision*. Boston: Houghton Mifflin.

Cooper, J. M. (1977). *Classroom teaching skills: A handbook*. Lexington, MA: D.C. Heath.

Cooper, J. M., and Allen, D. W. (1971). *Microteaching: Selected papers—history and present status*. Washington, D.C.: Association of Teacher Educators.

Cornett, C. E. (1983). *What you should know about teaching and learning styles*. Bloomington, IN: Phi Delta Kappa Educational Foundation.

Cubberly, E. F. (1934). *Public education in the U.S.* New York: Houghton Mifflin.

Curry, L. (1990). A critique of the research on learning styles. *Educational Leadership, 48* (2), 50–56.

Decline of 'traditional' families continued in '80s (1991, January 30). *The Free Press*, p. 5.

Devor, J. W. (1964). *The experience of student teaching*. New York: MacMillan.

Dinkmeyer, D., McKay, G. D., and Dinkmeyer, D., Jr. (1980). *STET—Systematic training for effective teaching (Leader's Manual)*. Circle Pines, MN: American Guidance Services.

Dobson, J. (1970). *Dare to discipline*. Wheaton, IL: Tyndale House Publishers.

Doll, R. C. (1986). *Curriculum improvement: Decision making and process* (6th edition). Boston: Allyn & Bacon.

Dreikurs, R., and Cassell P. (1972). *Discipline without tears* (2nd edition). New York: Hawthorn/Dutton.

Duke, D. L., and Meckel, A. M. (1984). *Teacher's guide to classroom management*. New York: Random House.

Dunn, R. (1990). Rita Dunn answers questions on learning styles. *Educational Leadership, 48* (2), 15–19.

Dunn, R., and Dunn, K. (1978). *Teaching students through their individual learning styles*. Reston, VA: Reston Publishing.

Dunn, R., Dunn, K., and Price, G. (1975, 1979, 1981, 1985, 1989). *Learning style inventory*. Lawrence, KS: Price Systems.

Dupuis, A. (1966). *Philosophy of education in historical perspective*. Chicago: Rand McNally.

Eisner, E. W. (1982). An artistic approach to supervision. In Thomas J. Sergiovanni (Ed.), *Supervision of teaching* (pp. 53–66). Association for Supervision and Curriculum Development.

Ernst, K. (1972). *Games students play (and what to do about them)*. Millbrae, CA: Celestial Arts.

Flanders, N. (1967). *Analyzing teacher behavior*. Reading, MA: Addison-Wesley.

Franck, M. R., and Samaniego, F. A. (1981). The supervision of teaching assistants: A new use of videotape. *Modern Language Journal, 65* (3), 273–280.

Freed, A. M. (1976). *T.A. for teens (and other important people)*. Sacramento, CA: Jalmar Press.

Furst, N., Sandefur, J. T., Bressler, A. A., and Johnston, D. P. (1971). *Interaction analysis: Selected papers*, Research Bulletin Number 10. Washington, D.C.: Association of Teacher Educators.

Gage, N. L., and Berliner, D. (1988). *Educational psychology*. Boston: Houghton Mifflin.

Galloway, C. (1962). *An exploratory study of observational procedures for teacher nonverbal communication*, Unpublished doctoral dissertation. Gainsville: University of Florida.

Gay, L. R. (1980). *Educational evaluation and measurement*. New York: Charles E. Merrill.

Glasser, W. (1965). *Reality therapy, a new approach to psychiatry*. New York: David McKay.

Glickman, C. D. (1990). *Supervision of instruction: A developmental approach*. Needham Heights, MA: Allyn & Bacon.

Goldhammer, R., Anderson, R. H., and Krajewski, R. J. (1980). *Clinical supervision: Special methods for the supervision of teachers*. New York: Holt, Reinhart & Winston.

Goodman, E. (1988, June 7). Intact single-parent families. *The Free Press* (Mankato, MN) p. 5.

Gordon, T. (1974). *T.E.T.—Teacher effectiveness training*. New York: David McKay.

Greene, B. (1991, January 12). Tale of hospital theft has a familiar ring. *The Free Press* (Mankato, MN), p. 5.

Greene, B. (1991, January 31). "Festival" seating is a dangerous sign of greed. *The Free Press* (Mankato, MN), p. 5.

Greene, M. (1967). *Existential encounters for teachers*. New York: Random House.

Gregorc, A. (1978, 1982). *Gregoric style delineator*. Maynard, MA: Gabriel Systems.

Gruber, F. C. (1973). *Historical and contemporary philosophies of education*. New York: Crowell.

Gursky, D. (1989, November). The demo man. *Teacher Magazine*, 62–63.

Haines, A. C. (Ed.). (1962). The outlook in student teaching. *The Association of Student Teaching 41st Yearbook*. Dubuque, IA: William C. Brown.

Haley, A., and Malcom X. (1964). *The Autobiography of Malcolm X*. New York: Grove Press, p. 95.

Hand, K. L. (1990). Style is a tool for students too! *Educational Leadership*, 48 (2), 13–14.

Harvey, O. J., Hunt, D. E., and Schroder, H. M. (1961). *Conceptual systems and personality organization*. New York: John Wiley & Sons.

Henry, M. A., and Beasley, W. W. (1989). *Supervising student teachers the professional way*. Terre Haute, IN: Sycamore Press.

Hill, J. E., and Nunnery, D. N. (1973). *The educational sciences*. Bloomfield Hills, MI: Oakland Community College Press.

Hodgkinson, H. (1990, April). Minnesota's future is here today. *Setting the Stage for the 21st Century: Proceedings of the Q7 Convocation*. The Minnesota State University System, 13–21.

Holmes Group. (1986). *Tomorrow's teachers*. East Lansing, MI.

Horton, L., and Harvey, K. (1979). Preparing cooperating teachers: The role of the university supervisor. *Peabody Journal of Education, 57* (1), 56–60.

Hunter, M. (1967). *Retention theory for teachers.* El Segundo, CA: TIP Publications.

Hunter, M. (1971). *Teach for transfer.* El Segundo, CA: TIP Publications.

Hunter, M. (1982). *Mastery teaching.* El Segundo, CA: TIP Publications.

Jackson, J. (1990, December). Black-on-black crime must end. *Minneapolis Star-Tribune,* p. 16A.

Johnson, J. A., and Perry, F. (1969). *Readings in student teaching.* Dubuque, IA: Kendall Hunt.

Johnson, M. (1967). Definitions and models in curriculum theory. *Educational Theory, 17* (2), 130.

Jones, R. C. (1970). University supervisor: A student teacher's best friend. *The Clearing House, 44* (7), 433.

Jones, V. F. (1980). *Adolescents with behavior problems—Strategies for teaching, counseling, and parent involvement.* Boston: Allyn & Bacon.

Joyce, B., and Well, M. (1988). *Models of teaching.* Englewood Cliffs, N.J.: Prentice-Hall.

Kagan, D. M. (1991). Builders of wooden boats and the reform of teacher education: A parable. *Phi Delta Kappa, 72* (9), 675–677.

Kagan, J. (1965). Reflection impulsivity and reading ability in primary grade children. *Child Development, 36,* 609–628.

Keefe, J. W., and Monk, J. S. (1988). *Learning style profile technical manual.* Reston, VA: National Association of Secondary School Principals.

Kneller, G. F. (1964). *Introduction to the philosophy of education.* New York: John Wiley & Sons.

Knight, G. F. (1982). *Issues and alternatives in educational philosophy.* Berrien Springs, MI: Andrews University Press.

Kolb, D. (1976). *Learning style inventory.* Boston: McBer.

Lang, D. C, Quick, A. F., and Johnson, J. A. (1981). *A partnership for the supervision of student teachers.* DeKalb, IL: Creative Educational Materials.

Lewis, A. (1990, July 9). When the U.S. fails its children. *Minneapolis Star-Tribune,* p. 12A.

Lindsey, M. (1969). *Inquiry into teaching behavior of supervisors in teacher education laboratories.* New York: Teachers College Press.

MacNaughton, R., Johns, F., and Rogus, J. (1978). Alternative models for revitalizing the school-university partnership. *Action in Teacher Education, 1,* 18–29.

McCarthy, B. (1990). Using the 4MAT system to bring learning styles to schools. *Educational Leadership, 48* (2), 31–37.

McGeogh, D. (1967, October). Helping student teachers become students of teaching. *Teachers College Journal, 39*, 18–21.

McKenney, J. L., and Keen, P. G. W. (1974). How managers' minds work. *Harvard Business Review, 52*, 79–90.

McNeil, J. D. (1982). A scientific approach to supervision. In Thomas J. Sergiovanni (Ed.), *Supervision of teaching*, Alexandria, VA: Association for Supervision and Curriculum Development, 18–34.

Major, R. L. (1981, Spring). Teacher-made tests . . . a brief review. *Private School Quarterly*, 9–10.

Major, R. L. (1984). Praise—an often overlooked tool of internal communication. *Journal of Educational Public Relations, 7* (1), 28–29.

Major, R. L. (1990). *Discipline: The most important subject we teach.* Lanham, MD: University Press of America.

Mallory, R. M. (1980). *Discipline in the classroom—the least approach.* Washington, D.C.: National Education Association.

Mann, H. (1844). *Fourth annual report: Covering the year 1840.* Boston: Dutton & Wentworth.

Mann, R. D. (1970). *The college classroom: Conflict, change and learning.* New York: John Wiley & Sons.

Marrou, J. R. (1988). The university supervisor: A new role in a changing workplace. *The Teacher Educator, 24* (3), 13–19.

Meierdiercks, K. (1981). Supervision and the videotape recorder. *NASSP Bulletin, 65*, (488) 30–41.

Merriman, P., and Fair, G. M. (1953). *Helping student teachers through evaluation*, Bulletin No. 2. Association for Student Teaching.

Morris, V. (1966). *Existentialism in education: What it means.* New York: Harper & Row.

Meyers, I. Briggs, and Briggs, K. C. (1943, 1976). *Myers-Briggs type indicator.* Palo Alto, CA: Consulting Psychologists Press.

National Education Association. *Today's Education.* (1987). Washington, D.C., *6*, 23.

National Institute of Justice Reports. (1990, January/February). No. 218. Rockville, MD.

National Institute of Justice Reports. (1990 Summer). No. 221. Washington, D.C., p. 35.

National School Safety Center. (1986). *School discipline notebook.* Sacramento, CA: Pepperdine University Press and the National School Safety Center.

National School Safety Center. (1988). *Drug traffic and abuse in school* (resource paper).

National School Safety Center. (1989). *Educated public relations 101.* Pepperdine University Press.

National School Safety Center. (1990, Winter). *School safety.*

Nelson, L., and McDonald, B. (1958). *Guide to student teaching.* Dubuque, IA: William C. Brown.

Nerenz, A. G. (1979). The role of the university supervisor: Perceived importance and practical implications. *Foreign Language Annals, 12* (6), 471–475.

New crime trend: killing for coats. (1990, December 12). *The Free Press,* (Mankato, MN), p. 3.

Niemeyer, R. C., and Moon, R. (1978). *Discovering supervisors' thought patterns through journals.* ERIC Document ED 281 840.

Office of Juvenile Justice and Delinquency Prevention. (1984). *Report of the N.I.J.J.D.P. fiscal years 1983–1984.* Washington, D.C.

Oja, S. N. (1988). *Some promising endeavors in school-university collaboration: Collaborative research and collaborative supervision in the University of New Hampshire five year program.* Paper presented at the Holmes Group Second Annual Conference, Washington, D.C., January 20–31, 1988. ERIC Document Number ED 294 835.

Oliva, P. F. (1988). *Developing the curriculum* (2nd edition). Glenview, IL: Scott Foresman.

Oliva, P. F. (1989). *Supervision for today's schools.* White Plains, NY: Longman.

O'Neil, J. (1990). Findings of styles research murky at best. *Educational Leadership, 48* (2), 7.

O'Neil, J. (1990). Link between style, culture proves divisive. *Educational Leadership, 48* (2), 8.

Owings, T. G., and Reitzammer, A. F. (1991). *Roles and responsibilities of directors of field experiences: A national study.* Tuscaloosa: University of Alabama.

Patterson, A., McGeogh, D., and Olson, H. (1979). *A brief history of the association for teacher educators.* Washington, D.C.: Association for Student Teaching.

Perrin, J. (1990). The learning styles project for potential dropouts. *Educational Leadership, 48* (2), 23–24.

Perrodine, A. F. Ed. (1955). The development of laboratory schools in teacher education. *The Association for Student Teaching 34th Yearbook.* Lockhaven, PA: Association for Student Teaching.

Raths, J., and Leepers, R. R., Ed. (1966). *The supervisor: Agent for change in teaching.* Washington, D.C.: Association for Supervision and Curriculum Development.

Reitzammer, A. F. (1991). The cooperating teacher: selection, training, and retention. *College Student Journal, 25* (1), 448.

Resnick, L. B. (1987). *Education and learning to think.* Washington, D.C.: Academy Press.

Rising Hispanic dropout rate worries educators. (1991, January 12). *The Free Press* (Mankato, MN), p. 3.

Rush, G., and Wood, J. (1982, Fall). In-service education of teacher educators: a national survey. *Action in Teacher Education, 4,* 71–73.

Scholl, R. L. (1990). *University supervisor: Circuit rider or teacher educator?* Paper presented at the Annual Meeting of the Association of Teacher Educators, Las Vegas, February 5–8, 1990. ERIC Document Number ED 317 506.

Schrader, G. (Ed.). (1967). *Existential philosophers: Kierkegaard to Merleau-Ponty.* New York: McGraw-Hill.

Sears, J. B. (1928). *Classroom organization and control.* Boston: Houghton Mifflin.

Seeley, L. (1903). *A new school management.* New York: Hinds & Noble.

Shanahan, D. (1990, November 25). Metal detectors for school's use to be discussed. *Sunday Omaha World-Herald,* p. 10.

Shipman, S., and Shipman, V. (1985). Cognitive styles: Some conceptual, methodological and applies issues. In E. H. Gordon (Ed.), *Review of education research.* Washington, D.C.: American Educational Research Association.

Shulman, L. S. (1987). Knowledge and teaching: Foundations of the new reform. *Harvard Educational Review, 57* (1), 1–22.

Simmons, J. M. (1988). "Wha'd she think?"—*A comparison of the role perspectives, evaluative judgment criteria cognitive maps, written records of three university student teacher supervisors.* Paper presented at the Annual Meeting of the American Educational Research Association, New Orleans, April 5–9, 1988. ERIC Document Number ED 293 808.

Simon, A., and Boyer, E. (Ed.). (1970). *Mirrors for behavior II: An anthology of observation instruments.* Philadelphia: Research for Better Schools.

Smart, W. E. (1986, October 19). Opinions split on job's value to a student. *Minneapolis Star-Tribune,* pp. 1F, 6F.

Smith, B. O., and Meux, M. O. (1962). *A study of the logic of teaching.* U.S. Department of Health, Education and Welfare, Office of Education, Cooperative Research Project No. 258. Urbana, IL: Bureau of Educational Research, College of Education, University of Illinois.

Smith, W. R. (1924). *Constructive school discipline.* New York: American Book Company.

Sobol, T. (1990) Understanding diversity. *Educational Leadership, 48* (3), 27–30.

Southwest Texas State University. (1987). *Classroom management and discipline program manual—A modular text*. San Marcos, TX: Classroom Management and Discipline Program, Lyndon B. Johnson Institute for the Improvement of Teaching and Learning, School of Education.

Sprick, R. S. (1985). *Discipline in the secondary school, a problem-by-problem survival guide*. West Nyack, NY: Center for Applied Research in Education.

Stewart, J. K. (1989, July/August). *N.I.J. Reports*. Number 215.

Study finds 1 in 8 U.S. kids hungry. (1991, March 26). *The Free Press* (Mankato, MN), p. 12.

Taba, H. (1962). *Curriculum development, theory and practice*. New York: NY: Harcourt, Brace and Jovanovich.

Teens who work may start ignoring real job: school. (1990, December 20). *Sunday Omaha World-Herald*, p. 1G.

Troyer, M. B. (1986). A synthesis of research on the characteristics of teacher educators. *Journal of Teacher Education, 37* (5), 6–11.

Uhlig, G., and Haberman, M. (1987). *A study of faculty development practice in schools, colleges and departments of education*. ERIC Research/Technical Report, Document Number ED 289 857.

U.S. Bureau of Labor Statistics. (1988, November 6). *Sunday Omaha World-Herald*, p. 16A.

Valverde, L. A. (1982). The self-evolving supervisor. In Thomas J. Sergiovanni (Ed.), *Supervision of teaching*. Association for Supervision and Curriculum Development 81–89.

Walcott, H. B. (Ed.). (1969). *Improving educational assessment and an inventory of measures of affective behavior*. Washington, D.C.: Association for Supervision and Curriculum Development.

Walk, J. E. (1917, October). Practice teaching and observation in normal schools. *Education, 39*, 69–85.

White, E. (1893). *School management*. New York: American Book Company.

Wiles, J., and Bondi, J. (1989). *Curriculum development: A guide to practice*. Columbus, OH: Merrill.

Williams, E. F. I. (1942). *The actual and potential use of laboratory schools in state normal schools and teacher colleges* (Contributions of Education, # 846, Bureau of Publications). New York: Columbia University Teachers College.

Wisconsin Center for Educational Research News. (1984). Madison, p. 6.

Witkin, H. A. (1976). Cognitive style in academic performance and in teacher-student relations. In *Individuality in learning*, Samuel Messick and Associates.

Wolk, R. A. (Ed.). (1989, November). Is democracy destiny? *Teacher Magazine*, p. 6.

Zeichner, K. M., and Liston, D. P. (1987). Teaching student teachers to reflect. *Harvard Educational Review, 57* (1), 23–48.

Index

ABOUT THE AUTHORS

DEBRA J. ANDERSON is Associate Professor of Education, Supervisor of Student Teachers, and Director of Student Teaching and Certification at St. Olaf College in Minnesota.

ROBERT L. MAJOR is Professor of Curriculum and Instruction and Supervisor of Student Teachers at Mankato State University. He is also the author of *Discipline: The Most Important Subject We Teach* (1990).

RICHARD R. MITCHELL is Professor of Curriculum and Instruction and Supervisor of Student Teachers at Mankato State University.